Perfect Bridge

A Collection of Seasonal Poems
and Meditations

JoAnn Dekker

ISBN 978-1-63630-436-6 (Paperback)
ISBN 978-1-63630-437-3 (Hardcover)
ISBN 978-1-63630-438-0 (Digital)

All scriptures, unless otherwise stated, are taken from the New International Version of the Holy Bible.

Covenant Books, Inc.
11661 Hwy 707
Murrells Inlet, SC 29576
www.covenantbooks.com

In every season of life, there is a bridge to cross before we can get to the other side of the spiritual ravine where our journey with God can continue to move forward. Our sins separate us from God, and the person and work of Jesus Christ are what it takes to bridge that gap. We can be assured the bridge is trustworthy! The bridge plan was engineered and executed by the Creator of the universe. Through these poems and reflections on the truths we are given in the Holy Scriptures, I pray each reader is led by the Spirit to identify the gaps between themselves and God in every season of life. I also pray for faith to cross the perfect bridge—the Savior, Jesus Christ, who brings us safely to our Father.

Contents

Spring

Season of Singing

*Y*ou are spring, and you are a welcome guest indeed!
Who can resist your mild manners and warmth of smile?
You bring us pleasure with your tender green array.
You please our senses with your fragrant blossoms fair.
You tease us with changing moods and indecision.
Full of life and promise, you are young and so sweet.
Your love song is carefree, bringing joy to our hearts.

The Gospel of Spring

(Song of Solomon 2:11–13)

When springtime arrives, the whole earth is filled with joy. Psalm 118:24 states, "This is the day that the Lord has made; let us rejoice and be glad in it." I like to start my days with this reminder to myself that each day is a gift! Each season is a gift, too, and spring has come! Song of Solomon 2:11–13 tells us, "See! The winter is past; the rains are over and gone. Flowers appear on the earth; the season of singing has come, the cooing of doves is heard in our land. The fig tree forms its early fruit; the blossoming vines spread their fragrance." We can anticipate these signs of spring because we know that our God is faithful!

We may love each season in its own right, for each has its own beauty and pleasures, but there is something about spring, isn't there? Nature resounds the greatest story ever told: that there is hope, there is life—there is life after death. There *must* be death before there can be life. So spring comes in the shadow of death. In the shadow of an old rugged cross. A seed is sown in righteousness, and our eyes are turned to Jesus, to the life spring of a resurrected savior. To Jesus, our death sacrifice, so there can be a life spring for us after death. Death cannot hold its prey, and death does not have the last word. Spring is a celebration of new life, of blossoming life, of the potential of life both now and in eternity.

Prayer: "I am not skilled to understand what God hath willed, what God hath planned. I only know at His right hand stands One who is my Savior. I take God at His word and deed. 'Christ died to save me'—this I read; and in my heart I find a need of Him to be my Savior. That He should leave His place on high, and come for sinful man to die, you count it strange? So do not I, before I knew my Savior. And oh that He fulfilled may see the travail of His soul in me, and with His work contented be, as I with my dear Savior! Yea, living, dying let me bring my strength, my solace from this spring: That He who lives to be my King, once died to be my Savior!" ("I Am Not Skilled to Understand," words of a hymn by Dora Greenwell, written in 1873). Amen.

The Way

(Matthew 7:13–14)

I stood still, transfixed, my gaze—pausing
to consider between two ways.
The roads ahead were clear to see—one led
to God, the other pleased me.
The first path looked smooth, the surroundings
fair. I was told there were no burdens
to bear.
I could indulge myself and in pleasure console. I would
be happy, healthy, and whole. Gratification would
mark the way. There would be no price to pay.
That second path looked treacherous and
steep. The journey seemed endless. I
began to weep.
I was told that my load would not be light. I
may have to travel through the dark
of night.
But I knew this road was marked with truth.
In God's word, I found my proof.
He said a Friend would bear the load. My
reward would be worth more than gold.
So I gave the first road one long last look.
The difficult road is the one I took.
Help has come each step of the way. On this road, I desire to stay.

I've been given a light to help me see. Others
have come to walk with me.
Sometimes I stumble, I know I could fall, but
when I look up, I hear God's call.
He beckons me on in sorrow or pain, promising
my loss will not match my gain.

Trials

Trials—they are the common denominator of the human condition. They come in so many different packages: physical, emotional, intellectual, relational, and financial. I believe they are all connected to our spiritual nature, though we may not recognize it at the time. "Consider it pure joy, my brothers, whenever you face trials of many kinds, because you know that the testing of your faith develops perseverance. Perseverance must finish its work so that you may be mature and complete, not lacking anything" (James 1:2–4). Wow! Pure joy! What a challenge! He goes on to say what we need to face those trials and how we get it: "If any of you lacks wisdom, he should ask God who gives generously to all without finding fault, and it will be given him. But when he asks, he must believe and not doubt, because he who doubts is like a wave of the sea, blown and tossed by the wind. That man should not think he will receive anything from the Lord; he is a double minded man, unstable in all he does" (James 1:5–8).

So what we need is wisdom and faith to believe God will give it and give generously. What kind of result can we expect when we face our trials in this way? James 1:12 states, "Blessed is the man who perseveres under trial, because when he has stood the test, he will receive the crown of life that God has promised to those who love him."

What a great reward is ours in Christ Jesus!

Prayer: As we persevere under our trials, Lord, give us wisdom and strength to consider it pure joy and to believe that, indeed, we can do all things—not in our own strength, but through You, Christ Jesus, our Savior, who gives us strength. Amen.

Should have, would have, could have, didn't
This is how to fret
It is what you'll want to do
If you like regret
Second-guess other chances
Consequence avoid
Weigh your options yet again
Until you're annoyed
Best to sit and think awhile
Don't get up and go
This way you can always say
"Guess we'll never know!"

No Excuses

Psalm 51 is a psalm written by King David after he was confronted with his sin of adultery with Bathsheba.

Psalm 51:1–12 states, "Have mercy on me, O God, according to your unfailing love; according to your great compassion blot out my transgressions. Wash way all my iniquity and cleanse me from my sin. For I know my transgressions, and my sin is always before me. Against you, you only, have I sinned and done what is evil in your sight, so that you are proved right when you speak and justified when you judge. Surely I was sinful at birth, sinful from the time my mother conceived me. Surely you desire truth in the inner parts; you teach me wisdom in the inmost place. Cleanse me with hyssop, and I will be clean; wash me, and I will be whiter than snow. Let me hear joy and gladness; let the bones you have crushed rejoice. Hide your face from my sins and blot out all my iniquity. Create in me a pure heart, O God, and renew a steadfast spirit within me. Do not cast me from your presence or take your Holy Spirit from me. Restore to me the joy of your salvation and grant me a willing spirit, to sustain me."

David prays for mercy; he confesses his sin is really against his God, who loves him. He chose to reject God's way. No excuses. David realizes his sin can separate him from the God that he loves, and he prays for forgiveness and restoration. He prays for the presence of the Holy Spirit to remain with him. Here is a quote, author unknown, that is so true: "If we cover our sin, God will expose it. If we expose our sin, God will cover it."

To what end, this restoration? Verses 13–17 says, "Then I will teach transgressors Your ways, and sinners will turn back to you. Save me from bloodguilt, O God, the God who saves me, and my tongue will sing of your righteousness. O Lord, open my lips, and my mouth will declare your praise. you do not delight in sacrifice, or I would bring it; you do not take pleasure in burnt offerings. The sacrifices of God are a broken spirit; a broken and contrite heart, O God, you will not despise."

There you have it. Sin, salvation, service; a life of thanksgiving and thanks living—to God's glory and to the benefit of others who can, in turn, also give glory to God. He alone is able to cleanse and restore.

Prayer: Lord, we know that those who mourn for their sin will be blessed, and they will be comforted. We pray that as we come to You in repentance, You will renew a right spirit in us and open the door for Your strength and power. I pray that those who have never known the freedom and forgiveness of confessed sin will find it. I also pray for those who *do* know that freedom—that they will find it again and again. Amen.

My Cry

When my heart aches so, and I don't know why
I ask You, Lord, to hear my cry
I know You love me, and I know You care
But I don't know how much You will ask me to bear
The source of this pain, I don't understand
But I'm reaching for You, please take my hand
In Your time, I ask that You dry all my tears
That You quiet my soul and calm all my fears
And when I've walked through to the other side
May I, in Your will, still safely abide

"Just Call Out My Name"

I love the Lord, for he heard my voice; he heard my cry for mercy. Because he turned his ear to me I will call on him as long as I live. The cords of death entangled me, the anguish of the grave came upon me; I was overcome by trouble and sorrow. Then I called on the name of the Lord: 'O Lord, save me!' The Lord is gracious and righteous; our God is full of compassion. The Lord protects the simple hearted; when I was in great need, he saved me. Be at rest once more, O my soul, for the Lord has been good to you. For you, O Lord, have delivered my soul from death, my eyes from tears, my feet from stumbling, that I may walk before the Lord in the land of the living." (Psalm 116:1–9)

Psalm 116 is my testimony. It is the testimony of all Christ followers, but it is personal for each of us. Pity the one who does not find himself entangled by death, trouble, or sorrow—or the one who has no idea who is able to deliver. I know that sounds wrong, but it is in trouble and sorrow that we realize our helplessness. If we don't recognize our needs, we don't look for a savior.

"Oh Lord, save me!"—and He did. He does. He will. My Deliverer has come, and He's coming again. I can and will live in trust. I can and will live in gratitude. "He has freed me from my chains" (Psalm 116:16b). He has freed me for His service. He has not only saved from death but has given reason to live. In the presence of others, I will praise the Lord, for when I was in great need, He saved me.

Prayer:

> My chains are gone
> I've been set free
> My God, my Savior has ransomed me
> And like a flood His mercy reigns
> Unending love, amazing grace.
> (Chorus from "Amazing Grace [My Chains
> Are Gone]" by Chris Tomlin)

Lord, hear this, my prayer, and this, my praise, in every trouble or sorrow of mine. And, Lord, hear this, my prayer and my testimony, in every trouble and sorrow of those He has given me to love. Amen.

Morning Joy

Morning has broken; joy has returned
Peace floods my being; truths have been learned
Sorrow and grief do not weigh on me
Grace has been given, my blessings to see
Today is the day to lay aside what has passed
To forget what's gone by, to treasure what lasts

"I Am Willing"

The account of the healing of the leper in Mark 1:40–45 gives us precious insight into the heart of our Savior. In a seemingly hopeless situation, a man afflicted with leprosy acts in faith by humbling himself and begging on his knees for healing. He believes that Jesus is able, if willing, to heal him, to change the circumstances that he is unable to change himself. He believes that Jesus is able to make him clean.

The Bible tells us that Jesus was filled with compassion. What a marvelous thought. Three simple words were then spoken: "I am willing." Jesus touched the man and spoke into his life. "Be clean," He said. The leper was cured. Jesus was willing. Jesus is willing. Let us, like this leper, take it to Him on our knees, whatever it is—whatever dirt, whatever shame, whatever effects from our own brokenness, the brokenness of others, or the brokenness of the world we live in—and ask Him to make it clean because we cannot. Jesus responds to faith. "Be clean," He says to the leper. "Be clean," He says to you and me. Jesus is both the sacrificial offering for our cleansing and the priest that declares us clean. We are the cured—and once we experience the miracle of healing and redemption, we cannot keep quiet, so we offer our sacrifices of praise and service, for He is worthy, and we are worthy in Him!

Prayer: Oh Lord, thank You for showing us Your willingness. You were willing to humble Yourself to a broken and sinful world. You were compassionate. You were sacrificial. I believe that You see me in my broken, sin-sick state, and I believe that You are compassionate. I believe You are able to mediate for me. I believe You have the power to cleanse me from all my sin and heal all my diseases. I believe You can make me new and You can make me productive for Your glory now and for Your eternal glory in the perfect world to come. I believe. Dispel any unbelief in me. Amen.

Obedient Mercy

When I can't seem to like, but love is the call
Help me to see You above it all
When another's burden looks too heavy to share
Call to my mind what Your strength can bear
If I'm tempted to calculate cost or pain
Let me consider Your cross, my gain
Remind me of Your footsteps to Calvary
Help me to follow You faithfully

Merciful Justice

How do You do that, God? How do You execute perfect justice and boundless mercy? In the book of Jeremiah, there is a prophecy of hope in the face of a needed sacrifice for sin—Jeremiah 5:3 says, "O Lord, do not your eyes look for truth?" Verse 12 says, "They have lied about the Lord, they said 'He will do nothing! No harm will come to us;'" That's what we sometimes do as well, don't we? That is what I have done. When God is looking for truth, I find that I have let the untruths of sin seep into my thoughts and rest in my heart. I have let myself rationalize or believe there does not need to be a consequence. But deep down, Lord, I know that isn't true. I deserve justice, I deserve consequence, and I deserve death. Sin separates from You, and separation from you is death, for You are the giver and sustainer of life. You are a God who demands justice, and there is no compromise that could give You the glory that You deserve. Yet I ask for mercy—and You give me mercy—the only *just* way.

Jeremiah 23:5 says, "The days are coming," declares the Lord, "when I will raise up from David's line a righteous Branch, a King who will reign wisely, and do what is just and right in the land." Verse 6B states, "This is the name by which he will be called: 'The Lord, Our Righteousness.'" Listen to Romans 3:21–25a: "But now a righteousness from God, apart from the law, has been made known, to which the Law and the Prophets testify. This righteousness from God comes through faith in Jesus Christ to all who believe. There is no difference, for all have sinned and fall short of the glory of God, and are justified freely by His grace through the redemption that came by Christ Jesus. God presented him as a sacrificed of atonement, through faith in His blood. He did this to demonstrate His justice," So I can hold my head up, but I can only do it if my eyes are fixed on Jesus, my Redeemer. I am released, but like one set free from prison, I can choose to still live with guilt and punish myself, or I can live in confidence that my debt has been paid. I do not have to bind myself to that prison of shame anymore or let Satan or any person keep me bound! That is how You do it, God—through Jesus, the Lord, our righteousness. God's prophecy in Isaiah is fulfilled! God's mercy, come in the flesh. Perfect justice satisfied by *His* sacrifice on my behalf. Mercy has been granted for me and can be granted for all who trust in the accomplished work of Jesus Christ. Life is all about Him. That is as it should be, the way it was always meant to be.

Prayer: Lord, God—You made a way for us! You made a way for our sentence to be lifted, for our lives to be ransomed, and for our freedom to be granted. We give You all the glory and all the praise. May our lives be a living sacrifice acceptable to You. In Your eyes, we are clean through our representative, Jesus, who justly satisfied the curse of death for the price of sin for all who believe. Help us to live in the joy of our forgiveness, the joy of You, our Lord and Savior. Amen.

Jesus

I said I would be with you, what still causes doubt?
I said, "Come unto me"; you want another way out
I told you of the strength you'd have if you would look to Me
Providing light upon your path and open eyes to see
You wonder what to do; you worry what to say
If you would just remember how I asked you first to pray
I will forgive your sin and offer you My grace
Lift your eyes above and look upon My face
I will wipe away your tear, and changing wrong to right
I will gladly calm your fear, just give to Me your fight
In Me are treasures of joy untold
Just reach out your hand for Me to hold
Remember I came, your burdens to bear
Your heartaches to heal, each want and each care
So bring Me all your heart's concern and bring Me all your need
Then when I break your chains of past, you will be free indeed

King Jesus

Mark 15:15–39 is an account of the events surrounding the crucifixion of the Lord Jesus Christ. The rejection of the one who came to bring light to show us the way of truth—to save us—is heartbreaking. It should be heartbreaking anyway—unless our hearts are hardened, as were the hearts of many at the time of His coming.

The kingship of Jesus, my precious Savior, was mocked then. The kingship of Jesus is also mocked now. Whoever does not believe in their hearts and confess with their mouths that Christ is Lord mocks His kingship. Each day, we have a choice to bow the knee in homage to the King or to mock his Lordship by refusing to respect His position of authority over our priorities, over our relationships, and over our self-will. Jesus Christ is not a king or ruler as our world is accustomed to. Jesus is a different kind of king. Listen to some of the lyrics quoted from singer-songwriter Katie Kapteyn DeGraff's Christmas album, "A different kind of king":

> You didn't come the way they thought you would, giving orders, swinging swords and wearing gold, You didn't show up in procession or parade, rather sung in by angels and by prophets foretold. Thorns instead of gold, a cross and not a throne. A wanderer with no palace, even faced your death alone. So better think the way He

really came—supernatural, holy, set apart. I'm left to realize the One I stand before. The Savior of the World, the King of my heart—A king that showed us love through doubt. A king that stood for justice on His knees. A king that believed in serving the least and undeserving, breathing life into you and into me—a different kind of king.

Matthew 10:32 states, "Whoever acknowledges me before others, I will also acknowledge before my Father in heaven."

And Matthew 7:21 says, "Not everyone who says to me, 'Lord, Lord,' will enter the kingdom of heaven, but only he who does the will of my Father who is in heaven."

Prayer: Father, even as your precious Son prayed, "Into Thy hands I commend my spirit," so may we commend our spirits, our lives, and our hearts to You. The one who did not spare Your only Son, but gave Him as a sacrifice for our sins; that in believing, we might have eternal life. Amen.

Love Does

Love lives, love gives
Love's tie won't die
Love spoken, chains broken
Love's hoping help's coping
Love's luring, love's enduring
Love humbles, pride crumbles
Love bends, love mends
Love's zeal, love's appeal
Love
Destroys the hateful, creates the grateful
Love's satisfaction
Is
A
Chain
Reaction

Love Appeal

(PHILEMON)

Love has appeal. Love is pretty irresistible. "Love comes from God. Everyone who loves has been born of God, and knows God" (1 John 4:7b).

Philemon, a Christian, loves his fellow Christians—the church that meets in his home. His love is an expression of the faith he has in Jesus, and it gives Paul, this letter-writer, great joy and encouragement to see that love at work. Paul's prayer for Philemon is that he would actively share his faith. Why? So that Philemon would have a full understanding of every good thing he had in Christ. Romans 10:9 states, "That if you confess with your mouth, 'Jesus is Lord,' and believe in your heart that God raised him from the dead you will be saved. For it is with your heart that you believe and are justified, and it is with your mouth that you confess and are saved."

When we learn something, we may know it, but there is something about communicating what is known to others that solidifies it. Knowledge becomes transformed into faith. I think it's that fuller understanding and deeper faith that brings a person to a place of gratitude.

On the basis of Philemon's love, Paul appeals to him on behalf of a former slave of Philemon's, Onesimus. Onesimus apparently left Philemon, became a believer, and was serving Paul while he was in prison. Paul does not want to offend Philemon by keeping Onesimus and is writing to let Philemon know he is sending him back. Paul asks Philemon to accept him as a brother and a partner in the work of the church, not as the slave he formerly was. Paul is pretty confident that Philemon will be obedient to do what he asks. That's the appeal of love. That's the response of love. That's what we do. We love, and we watch in faith to see what that love appeal will do.

Prayer: Lord, help us to be like Paul to look not only to our own needs but also to the needs of others. As your love is irresistible to us, help us to actively share our faith in love so we will have a full understanding of every good thing we have in You, Christ Jesus, who showed us that "Love never fails." I Corinthians 13:8a. Amen.

Forgiveness

Who am I to bear a grudge, to deny the way to mend?
Who am I to withhold my grace, to stiffly refuse to bend?
Wasn't it me who on mercy called when lost upon my way?
Wasn't I the one who was granted Your forgiveness on that day?
Wasn't it You who showed Your love could wash me clean like rain?
Wiping away the filth and grime, with no trace of stain?
A hypocrite, I will not be; forgiveness, I now know.
I won't deny Your love in me, so mercy I will show.

Forgiveness Is Not an Option

(Matthew 18:21–35; James 2:13; Colossians 3:13; Ephesians 4:32)

Isn't it great that God gave us such clear, black-and-white instructions on the subject of forgiveness? No gray area here. Perhaps it's because God knows how hard this can be and how fundamental this is to relationships. He knows better than anyone, doesn't He? Nobody sacrificed more for the sake of forgiveness than God through the sacrifice of His Son, Jesus, or Jesus through His obedience to His Father's will.

Out of God's great love, forgiveness is offered through the sacrifice of our Lord Jesus Christ. Out of God's great love, forgiveness is given through faith in this same Lord Jesus Christ. Out of God's great love, He asks us to forgive. Our human nature tries to convince us that we have a right to a grudge—after all, our pain deserves some justice, and the person who caused our pain deserves some retribution. James 2:13 tells us that mercy triumphs over justice and judgment without mercy will be shown to anyone who has not been merciful. We would be lost without God's mercy given in Jesus Christ who served justice on our behalf. Mercy triumphed for us, and mercy must triumph through us. Thanks be to God who sets us free and gives us the power to set free the one who is indebted to us. Justice was served for all who believe in Christ. As for those who do not believe or those who are unrepentant? That is between them and God. But our willingness to forgive and extend mercy to others is between us and God.

Prayer: The concept of forgiveness seems easy when we need forgiveness, but the act of forgiveness when it requires us to sacrifice our sense of justice is not always so easy, Lord. Please don't let us forget about the debt we could not pay when we are thinking about someone's debt to us, and help us to remember that You are the judge.

Devotion

To what are you devoted? To what will you be true?
What is so important that it matters more than you?
Is there something that you thought you needed
or at least that's what was told,
But it turned out it wasn't all it seemed, and left you feeling cold?
Are you reluctant to release your grasp on what you think you've earned?

Then I guess that there is a lesson that still needs to be learned.

The things in this world are fleeting and come at such a cost,
But what you get when you give them up far outweighs their loss.
So be willing to end your futile strife on things that will not last.
Devote yourself to Jesus, your hopes on Him to cast.
Put your effort in His kingdom work though reward's not clearly seen.
A harvest of eternal blessing, I know you'll surely glean.

Dog Love

I have a dog right now that brings me a lot of joy. I have had other dogs—each of them with characteristics I have also enjoyed or appreciated, but I said of this dog the other day, "All he really seems to live for is to love and to be loved." My dog is easy to love. He wants to please me; he is affectionate to me and readily accepts with gratitude my affection for him. He loves me best, but he is always ready to show love to anyone, whether he knows them or not.

I started to think about that and thought, *It's that simple with us and God. He created us to be objects of His love, and we were created to respond to that love—to love Him back and to love others as an outlet of His love overflowing in us. In this love, He is glorified.*

Listen to the Bible as I read a few verses taken from the book of 1 John 4 verse 7: "Dear friends, let us love one another, for love comes from God. Everyone who loves has been born of God, and knows God." Verse 19: "We love because he first loved us." Verse 15 to 16: "If anyone acknowledges that Jesus is the Son of God, God lives in him, and he in God. And so we know and rely on the love God has for us. God is love. Whoever lives in love, lives in God, and God in him."

I know the love and devotion my dog has for me lacks the depth and capacity of the love relationship between God and us, but it is a reminder to keep it simple! It's all about God, and God is love. How do you want to respond to His love today?

Prayer: "I love you, Lord, and I lift my voice to worship You—oh my soul, rejoice! Take joy my king in what You hear—let it be a sweet, sweet sound in Your ear!" (Laurie Klein) Amen.

Come Closer

Come closer, My love, I've called your name
Come take My hand, you'll be glad you came
Come closer, My love, you'll see My power
Sufficient for life, each day, each hour
Come closer, My love, I'll speak words to you
Of a perfect love that's forever true
Come closer, My love, I'll breathe breath in you;
My breath has life to make all things new
Come closer, My love, when all else fades away; My
glory you will see on the morn of that new day

Intimacy

(2 Chronicles 7:14; James 4:1–11; Hebrews 4:16)

Do you know that God invites us to be intimate with Him? The thought brings tears to my eyes. Why would anyone reject or avoid intimacy with God? We do, you know. We reject and avoid intimacy—not only with God, but also in the relationships He has given us. We know ourselves, and we don't always want our true selves to be known. We sometimes get comfortable with our own deficiencies, finding it easy to be self-forgiving again and again without requiring any change of ourselves. Admitting our sins and failures to God or others requires humbling. It requires change. So with pride, we build a wall around ourselves and our sins, preventing true intimacy—perhaps deceiving ourselves into thinking we are entitled to keep things the same. After all, others hold on to their sins. We believe there is a benefit for us in our sin that outweighs the intimacy of total disclosure, admittance of wrong, and willingness to change. Acceptance of that lie is avoidance and rejection of intimacy with God.

God sees our walls. He knows what they are made of, and He knows why we have built them. He knows the sins and insecurities the walls are meant to protect. He also knows what it takes to break down the walls. He knew Jesus was the way to do it, and He can help us build new walls that protect from the enemy, instead of protecting for the enemy.

Oh, what we miss when we ignore the invitation to come close to God. Oh, how we deceive ourselves when we think God is safer at a distance. When He is close to us, we hear His voice. We see His power. We feel His breath, breathing life into our souls. "If my people, who are called by my name, will humble themselves and pray and seek my face and turn from their wicked ways, then will I hear from heaven and will forgive their sin and will heal their land" (2 Chronicles 7:14). "God opposes the proud but gives grace to the humble. Submit yourselves, then to God. Resist the devil, and he will flee from you. Come near to God and he will come near to you. Humble yourselves before the Lord, and he will lift you up" (James 4:6b, 7–8, and 10). "Let us then approach the throne of grace with confidence, so that we may receive mercy and find grace to help us in our time of need' (Hebrews 4:16).

Prayer: "Breathe on me, breath of God. Fill me with life anew, that I may love what thou dost love and do what thou wouldst do. Breathe on me Breath of God, so shall I never die, but live with Thee the perfect life, of Thine eternity" (hymn by Edwin Hatch, verses 1 and 4). Amen.

Why, God?

Why did You color the sky so blue with brushes of wispy white?
I think to myself, it just must be to give your child delight.
When You covered the hills in the calm of green
and dotted them with flowers fair,
You must have wanted to show this child how much You really care.
Why did You give birds songs to sing as they fly from tree to tree?
Such a joyful noise they bring; somehow I feel free.
You didn't have to give the rain that leaves the smell of earth
Or the aroma of an ocean breeze that somehow speaks my worth.
How velvety soft a petal to feel, how sweet the smell they bring.
In the presence of this that You have made, my soul wells up to sing.
These sacred moments You give to me are glimpses, Lord, of You,
So I thank You Lord for the love You show in all the things You do.

God's Love

(JOHN 3:16; PSALM 36:5–10; EPHESIANS 3:14–21)

Spring is often referred to as a season of love. It is a fitting time to turn our thoughts to scripture passages that pertain to God's amazing, unsurpassable love. The first Bible verse of focus is likely the most famous verse—often called the gospel or good news in a nutshell: "For God so loved the world that he gave his one and only Son, that whosoever believes in him should not perish, but have everlasting life" (John 3:16). God's love to us is demonstrated in His sacrifice.

Next is a selection from the book of Psalms. Psalm 36:5–10 states, "Your love, O Lord, reaches to the heavens, your faithfulness to the skies. Your righteousness is like the mighty mountains, your justice like the great deep. O Lord, you preserve both man and beast. How priceless is your unfailing love! Both high and low among men find refuge in the shadow of your wings. They feast on the abundance of your house; you give them drink from your river of delights. For with you is the fountain of life; in your light we see light." The implication is that God's love is limitless and immeasurable by human standards. Songwriter Frederick M. Lehman tries to give expression to the magnitude of God's love in the song "The Love of God." Stanza 1 proclaims, "The love of God is greater far than tongue or pen can ever tell." Stanza 3 states, "Could we with ink the ocean fill and were the skies of parchment made, were every stalk on earth a quill and every man a scribe by trade. To write the love of God above would drain the ocean dry. Nor could the scroll contain the whole, though stretched from sky to sky."

God is love! (1 John 4:8). God has many characteristics, but *He is love*! It is His example of love that we have to model. Isn't love what we all crave to have and to give? In His power, we, too, can have love—to live in His love and to show His love. Love is His gift to us. Let's receive it and give it with thanksgiving.

Prayer: "For this reason I kneel before the Father, from whom his whole family in heaven and on earth derives its name. I pray that out of his glorious riches he may strengthen you with power through his Spirit in your inner being, so that Christ may dwell in your hearts through faith. And I pray that you, being rooted and established in love, may have power, together with all the saints, to grasp how wide and long and high and deep is the love of Christ, and to know this love that surpasses knowledge—that you may be filled to the measure of all the fullness of God. Now to him who is able to do immeasurably more than all we ask or imagine, according to his power that is at work within us, to Him be glory in the church and in Christ Jesus throughout all generations, for ever and ever!" (Ephesians 3:14–21) Amen.

The Truth of God

The truth of God shall ever stand
Protected by His mighty hand
Though generations come and go
His own His truth will surely know
His truth shall stand above all lies
All powerful to save
His love and grace will reach beyond
The darkness of the grave

The Whole Truth, and Nothing but the Truth

What is truth anyway? Many people think it is whatever they believe. A synonym for truth is fact. Fact is generally agreed upon; it is something that is indisputable. That is to say—you cannot make a case or argument against it. Yet when it comes to the Bible, you will encounter those who do not believe it is true or factual. There are those who try to dispute it, and they are disputing God, who has revealed Himself through it. It comes down to this for each of us: we can believe what God says is truth, or we can believe a lie. Truth is indisputable for those who have faith; the Spirit of God testifies to it. There is no argument or case that can legitimately be made against it, for there is no argument that can be legitimately made against God. Eyes and hearts have either been opened to the truth or opened to untruth. Have your eyes been opened to the truth?

It all started with Adam and Eve, didn't it? God said to Adam, "You must not eat from the tree of the knowledge of good and evil. For when you eat of it you will surely die." That was truth. Adam and Eve had truth and life offered, but they wanted another option—to know about evil, to know untruth. They wanted more than what God had given them. They were deceived by a lie offered by the devil: that they would not surely die as God had said. Eve was deceived. Then she became a deceiver. That's the way it is with a lie. First you believe it, then by the way you live or the things you say, you try to get others to believe it.

The Bible tells us, "Do not be deceived, God is not mocked." What He says has come to pass, what He says is, and what He says will come to pass. Death has come from a lie believed; death does come from a lie believed, and death will come from a lie believed. Jesus said in His prayer to God in John 1:17, "Your word is truth." Jesus said in John 14:6, "I am the way, the truth, and the life. No one comes to the Father except through me." In John 8:43–44, Jesus says to the unbelieving Jews, "Why is my language not clear to you? Because you are unable to hear what I say. You belong to your father, the devil, and you want to carry out your father's desire. He was a murderer from the beginning, not holding to the truth, for there is no truth in him. When he lies, he speaks his native language, for he is a liar, and the father of lies."

When we believe what is contrary to what the Bible says, we step over to the enemy's team, choosing darkness over light, choosing lies over truth, and choosing a path to death rather than life. Wisdom is needed to tell the difference between lies and truth, for the devil is very crafty, and he will often take a little bit of truth to disguise the lie so it will be more believable. The good news is that God will give us that wisdom to discern if we ask and if we believe that He really is the source of wisdom and truth. Being very familiar with the truth will help us recognize lies. Memorizing and meditating on God's Word and asking God to write it on our hearts will guard us against lies.

Prayer: Father, we pray for wisdom to recognize the lies in the culture around us and in our own thoughts. Free us from deception by shedding Your light of truth on our paths and helping us to embrace it—for Your glory. Amen.

Spring Bridge

When in spring's youth you test what you were told
You don't think ahead; you're a little too bold
You may suddenly find the waters too deep
You're swimming in regret for taking that leap
My grace in forgiveness is the bridge to see
The way to bring you back to me.

Summer

Season of Growth

Oh, summer, we are grateful you have arrived!
We see your productive maturity.
The brightness of your smile sparkles through the leaves.
Your character is revealed in iridescent greens.
The gentle breath of your presence surrounding us.
We take refuge in the cooling shade of your garments.
Your song is bold, bringing peace and purpose to our souls.

Steps of Spiritual Growth

(PSALM 19:1–14)

In Psalm 19, David provides a kind of outline of the progression of faith and spiritual growth that takes place when someone becomes a believer in God. In verses 1 to 4a, the psalmist begins with creation: "The heavens declare the glory of God; the skies proclaim the work of his hands. Day after day they pour forth speech; night after night they display knowledge. There is no speech or language where their voice is not heard. Their voice goes out into all the earth, their words to the ends of the world." Who can look into the sky, at the moon and the stars, and at the sun rising and setting and not see the magnificence of a God behind it all? As the saying goes, a picture paints a thousand words and creation is a billion pictures of one wonder after another, speaking a language universal to all. Acknowledgment in the existence of a Creator-God is the first step of faith and the beginning of growth.

Verses 7 to 11 tells us, "The law of the Lord is perfect, reviving the soul. The statutes of the Lord are trustworthy, making wise the simple. The precepts of the Lord are right, giving joy to the heart. The commands of the Lord are radiant, giving light to the eyes. The fear of the Lord is pure, enduring forever. The ordinances of the Lord are sure and altogether righteous. They are more precious than gold, than much pure gold; they are sweeter than honey, than honey from the comb. By them is your servant warned; in keeping them there is great reward." There are a lot of words here that refer to God's Word or law through which God's righteousness and authority is revealed. Believing in the revelation of God's Word is another medium and step in spiritual growth. Believing that what He says is right, true, and perfect, and acknowledging that we miss that mark of perfection is the next step of spiritual growth.

In verses 12 to 14, the psalmist writes, "Who can discern his errors? Forgive my hidden faults. Keep your servant also from willful sins; may they not rule over me. Then will I be blameless, innocent of great transgressions. May the words of my mouth and the meditation of my heart be pleasing in your sight, O Lord, my Rock and my Redeemer." The psalmist expresses a desire to be forgiven and have a changed heart. That's where Jesus comes in! So you see as Alistair Begg once aptly summarized, God's *world* brings us to His *Word*, which brings us to His *will*. Where are you on this journey of spiritual growth? Is it time to take the next step?

Prayer: "Our Father, who art in heaven, hallowed be your name, Thy kingdom come, Thy will be done, on earth as it is in heaven. Give us this day our daily bread. And forgive us our debts, as we also have forgiven our debtors. Lead us not into temptation, but deliver us from evil, for yours is the kingdom, and the power, and the glory forever. Amen."

Blossoms

Brilliant colors fade to brown
As blossomed petals lay life down
Just a moment, this beauty of youth's prime
Enjoyed for oh so brief a time
For fruit to develop and begin to grow
These lovely flowers just have to go
For we know that all nature has been given a need
For the food that will nourish and then for its seed
Part of maturation is to gracefully give
For in the leaving behind, comes the purpose to live
All of life's cycles and seasons planned
Carefully guided by God's sovereign hand

Running to Walk

(Amos)

In the book of Amos, Israel, Judah, and surrounding nations were given prophesies to announce God's coming judgment for their sins. Scripture says that they were concerned only for their next drink while they crushed the poor and needy. God reminded Israel that He expected more from them—they were His family, His chosen—chosen to receive His law, His word, and His deliverance. In Amos 3, the question is asked by the Lord, "Do two walk together unless they have agreed to do so?" Israel was breaking covenant with God, and they were not walking with Him any longer.

We cannot walk with God if we have chosen our own direction. If we are not walking with God, we will move away from Him. God gave Israel a warning in His grace. He gives us a warning in His grace, calling us to seek Him, to seek good, and to hate evil so we might live. God's presence would go with Israel again, but not until they ran from evil to look for God's goodness and His presence. When we find ourselves walking our own way, it's time to run, and we've got to run back to God before we can walk with Him. Amos 5:20 states, "Will not the day of the Lord be darkness, not light—pitch dark, without a ray of brightness?" God says He does not want empty sacrifices, religious feasts or songs of praise. Amos 5:23 states, "Away with the noise of your songs! I will not listen to the music of your harps. But let justice roll on like a river, righteousness like a never-failing stream!"

In Amos chapter 9, God says that when He punishes Israel, it will be like grain shaken in a sieve. Not a pebble or a true kernel will be lost, but only sinners who do not believe the Word of the Lord will die by the sword. They will search for the Word of Lord that they rejected, but will not find it.

So the story of God's plans for mankind always ends well for those who come back to God—humbled and changed. They are promised permanent restoration. It's the ones who have run from sin to the Savior for forgiveness and restoration so they can walk with God.

Prayer: Lord, you have told us that if we want to love life and see good days we must keep our tongues from evil and deceitful speech, turn from evil and do good, seek peace and pursue it, for your eyes are on the righteous, and your ears attentive to their prayer, but your face is against those who do evil. Deliver us from evil in the name of Jesus, that we might walk with You (1 Peter 3:10–11). Amen.

Home

She looks so peaceful standing on the hill, a picture of tranquility...
Serene.
She looks as if she never saw shame or pain, neglect or abuse...
Content.
Seeing her is to imagine—no, to remember—
Lazy, barefoot summers filled with children's laughter;
Cozy, quiet winters with bedtime stories and "Love you" kisses;
Warm meals and scents of foods freshly baked;
Soft-spoken prayers and sweet songs sung to Jesus.
She does not speak of what was once there, the unwelcome destroyers.
Her bright lights have penetrated the darkness brought.
Time, effort, and grace conceal the flaws
that would diminish her beauty.
So I see her exactly as she appears—
Peaceful, serene,
Humble, clean,
Bright, and beautiful.
I remember her laughter, and I cherish her love.
Home.

Pressure Ulcer Intervention

(JEREMIAH 30:12–17)

As a nurse, I am familiar with pressure ulcers. As the term implies, they develop as a result of ongoing pressure that prevent tissues from getting blood flow, which is, of course, vital to tissue life. The severity of the wound and prognosis for recovery is based on how long exposure to the pressure occurs, the degree of the pressure, and the integrity of the skin and tissue to begin with. I have observed pressure ulcers in early stages merely look like a reddened area on the skin. Without intervention, these can progress to ugly wounds, which are opportunities for harmful bacteria to feed. They are rotting, often infecting, are difficult to heal, and sometimes life-threatening. It doesn't take as long as you might think to happen either!

There are all different types of pressures, aren't there? External circumstances that compromise us internally. It is most devastating when pressure erodes our spiritual integrity. Spiritual ulcers are the deadliest because they have eternal implications. The Bible describes such a wound that reminds me of a pressure ulcer and is incurred as a result of unrepentant sin. In Jeremiah 30:12–17, God prophesies through Jeremiah regarding the wound of sin that marked Israel as a nation. Hear these verses as follows: "This is what the Lord says: 'Your wound is incurable, your injury beyond healing. There is no one to plead your cause, no remedy for your sore, no healing for you. All your allies have forgotten you; they care nothing for you. I have struck you as an enemy would and punished you as would the cruel, because your guilt is so great and your sins so many. Why do you cry out over your wound, your pain that has no cure? Because of your great guilt and many sins I have done these things to you.'"

Israel could not find the remedy for their sin wounds any more than we can find a remedy for ours on our own. The good news is that God is able to provide that miracle intervention, that healing we cannot find. Read verse 17a: "'But I will restore you to health and heal your wounds,' declares the Lord." It continues on to these beautiful words in verse 21b and 22: "'I will bring him near and he will come close to me, for who is he who will devote himself to be close to me?' declares the Lord. 'So you will be my people, and I will be your God.'"

Has He opened your heart to hear His Word to see your wounds at whatever stage they are and to ask for His intervention?

Prayer: We are unable to heal our sin wound, so, Jesus, we look to You in faith to heal us with Your life-giving blood, transfused to all who see their need, saving from soul's death.

He's Real All Right

He's real all right—
Although I suppose there are sources of greater credibility than me.
But I can tell you, I felt his presence, and I was
physically cold; I was chilled to my
very soul.
I was drawn into his darkness. He offered me
comfort, but of course, he is a liar.
Yes, I saw him. In places, in people, and in the people I
love. They were changed by him. Even physically changed
in their affect—in their eyes, they were liars too.
I, myself, began to waste away when I entertained his
company. I loathed my life. I became obsessed with the
evil that surrounded me, enveloped me. Pleasure eluded
me and excluded me. I was inclined toward hatred.
I heard him. In the voices of others, in the voices
in my head; those lies again, over
and over they played in my mind. For a time,
I was reluctant to exchange them for
the truth, unready to shut them out, as if I were
challenging the tempter to persuade
me to listen to his voice
His touch removed me from my own familiarity.
There was a heightened awareness
of something going on outside of myself as if I
were being lifted into the realm of the
spirits, and I no longer knew how to talk, how to
act, and how to go on with this thing

called human life.
So we did battle, he and I. In the activity of the
day and in the still of the night, we
fought our private fight. In the end, I prevailed.
In the strength of Another, I
claimed my victory, for He gave to me a power
I did not possess. That source of
light and life and truth—
That source of greater credibility.
He's real all right.

Strength in God's Armor

(EPHESIANS 6:10–18)

How can you be strong when you're tired and weak? Where do you find power when you realize you are powerless? How do you find a defense when you know you are defenseless? Security when you are vulnerable? Protection when under assault?

I was reading in the book of Ephesians recently, and it is here that God gives us the answer: "Finally, be strong in the Lord and in his mighty power. Put on the full armor of God so that you can take your stand against the devil's schemes. For our struggle is not against flesh and blood, but against the rulers, against the authorities, against the powers of this dark world and against the spiritual forces of evil in the heavenly realms. Therefore put on the full armor of God, so that when the day of evil comes, you may be able to stand your ground, and after you have done everything, to stand. Stand firm then, with the belt of truth buckled around your waist, with the breastplate of righteousness in place, and with your feet fitted with the readiness that comes from the gospel of peace. In addition to all this, take up the shield of faith, with which you can extinguish all the flaming arrows of the evil one. Take the helmet of salvation and the sword of the Spirit, which is the word of God. And pray in the Spirit on all occasions with all kinds of prayers and requests. With this in mind, be alert and always keep on praying for all the saints" (Ephesians 6:10–18).

Many times when we are facing struggles, we identify the things we see (people who oppose us, financial struggles, sins and failures, diseases, or the diseases of those we love or care about) as the enemy. Ephesians tells us that those are not our true enemy. Our struggle is not really against flesh and blood or the things we can see in the physical world. Our struggle is against the *spiritual* forces that are out to destroy us. The devil uses the physical things as weapons to get at our spirit. So how do we fight back? By using the spiritual things (the armor that God provides) to attack back! What a concept! What a revelation! What a challenge! What a comfort to know that God has not left us defenseless!

Prayer: Open our spiritual eyes, Lord, to see not only our enemy but the resources that are available to us in battle! You have said that the one who is in us is greater than the one who is in the world! The battle is ultimately Yours, and You have appointed us as ambassadors and warriors for your cause. We know that You will reign victorious and us with You! We know You are able to keep us from falling and to present us before Your presence without fault and with great joy (Jude 1:24)! We give You praise, and we give You thanks! Amen.

Summer's Ways

Adventure, fun
Relaxation, sun
Refresh, revive
Recreate, alive
Warm, free
World, see
Green, grand
Water, sand
Life, observed
People, served
Time, spent
Love, lent
Summer's days
Summer's ways

Spiritual Pruning

(JOHN 15:1–7)

I was pruning my trumpet vine the other day, and I was thinking about these words in John 1:1–2: "I am the true vine, and my Father is the gardener. He cuts off every branch in me that bears no fruit, while every branch that does bear fruit He prunes so that it will be even more fruitful."

It is a known fact that when a part of something living has died, it is often lifesaving to remove it so that what is alive can flourish. That is an occasion for pruning. In the case of my trumpet vine though, nothing was dead—on the contrary, the vine was flourishing. You see, the purpose of planting the trumpet vine was to enhance the arbor that provides an entrance for a walkway to the park behind my home. The vine, though, was not inclined to enhance the arbor—it wanted to take it over. In fact, it seemed to be trying to obscure the walkway altogether, blocking the entrance to the park. So in spite of the healthy appearance of the vine, I took my pruning shears and proceeded to cut away at it until nearly half of it was gone. The growth is now going to take a new direction—the direction it needs to take to fulfill the purpose for which it was planted.

God, our Master Gardener, fully knows the purpose for each believer's planting. Pruning must sometime occur in a believer's life even though, by all appearances, they might be productive and flourishing because they are not flourishing in the way that God intended. Don't be too concerned when God allows things to be taken from you or stops you in your path and turns you in another direction. He is just helping you to fulfill your purpose, and sometimes that means getting rid of what is not needed or what is moving you in the wrong direction. Remain in Christ Jesus, and your life will bear fruit—fruit that lasts. The Master Gardener will see to the pruning to keep you on track.

Prayer: Lord, pruning is very uncomfortable sometimes. Help us to be grateful that You know exactly what You are doing and to believe that we can bear fruit in the life-vine you provide in Christ Jesus.

Erica's Poem

(AUTHOR: ERICA OGDEN)

She walks, I follow—tender care, smiles, and first steps.
She teaches me well—help around the house,
play nicely with your sisters,
Obey your parents.
She walks—"Kids of the kingdom, that's what we are!"
"My name is Erica, and I love the Lord"
Take good care of others and
Offer your talents.
She walks, I follow—be a hard worker, take care of your blessings.
She teaches me well—do your best, say you're sorry, exercise,
Eat right.
She walks, I follow—plant flowers, make soup,
play games, eat chocolate and ice cream.
She teaches me well—give care to the sick and the
dying, be compassionate, save a dollar,
Share.
Take a hike, enjoy nature, snow ski, water ski,
study the Bible, do what it says.
Pray always.
Trust the Lord, believe, forgive, bear good fruit:
Love, joy, peace, patience, kindness,
Goodness, faithfulness,
Gentleness, and self-control.

I follow her as
She follows our Christ.
She walks, I follow.
Write a poem that's from the heart.
She teaches me well.

Of Shepherds and Sheep

(PSALM 23)

The Lord is my shepherd, I shall not want. He makes me lie down in green pastures, he leads me beside quiet waters. He restores my soul. He guides me in paths of righteousness for His name's sake. Even though I walk through the valley of the shadow of death, I will fear no evil; for you are with me your rod and your staff, they comfort me. You prepare a table before me in the presence of my enemies. You anoint my head with oil; my cup overflows. Surely goodness and love will follow me all the days of my life, and I will dwell in the house of the Lord forever. (Psalm 23)

David was a shepherd boy. It takes one to know one. David recognized the relationship he had with his sheep was like the relationship God had with him, and with His people. What does a shepherd provide? A shepherd provides protection, security, provision, restoration, guidance, comfort—all these things—so that our lives, like those of the sheep, can be fruitful. What do I have that David's sheep did not have? I am promised eternal dwelling in the house of the Lord because the Good Shepherd laid down His life for the sheep. The Shepherd became the lamb.

I am content. I am content to be one of His sheep because I am safe with Him. He would and did risk and relinquish His life to go after me, to save me from myself and my inclination to stray. How about you? Can you trust this Shepherd? Hasn't He proven Himself trustworthy?

Prayer: "Savior, like a shepherd lead us. Much we need thy tender care. In Thy pleasant pastures feed us. For Thy use Thy folds prepare. We are Thine, do thou befriend us. Be the guardian of our way. Keep Thy flock from sin defend us. Seek us when we go astray. Thou hast promised to receive us, poor and sinful though we be. Thou hast mercy to relieve us. Grace to cleanse, and power to free. Blessed Jesus, Blessed Jesus, Thou hast loved us, love us still. Blessed Jesus, blessed Jesus, Thou hast loved us, love us still" (words from a song by William B. Bradbury, "Savior like a Shepherd Lead Us").

Discontentment

She wakes me each day.
She's abrupt and she's cruel,
She scorns and she laughs
Because I am her fool.
She robs me of joy;
She instead gives me pain.
She deflects sun's rays,
Ushering in cold rain.
She is my shadow
From morning until night.
I protest intrusion;
She claims it is her right.
Like cancer she grows,
Recruits others along.
She is so deceiving,
Obsessing all wrong.
There is nothing lovely;
No, nothing is good.
These are the concepts that
She wants understood.
Discontentment, you are
Surely not my friend.
Plead I a new spirit—
Gratitude to send.

Griping Where You Are

(It Doesn't Get You Far)
(Numbers 11)

This Bible passage is such a great revelation about God and about human nature. It is human nature, I believe, to never be satisfied. It starts in infancy, when piercing cries from our bundles of joy protest discomfort or announce like an alarm in the middle of a moment of tranquility that there is a need that must be met. So it was with God's people in the book of Numbers. Delivered from the bondage of slavery, they began to recall that they did have some provision back in the day of slavery, and they began to voice resentment over that loss. What was God's response? Initially, God was angry because of their discontentment, and He sent fire that consumed some of the outskirts of their camp. God's show of power was followed by a cry for mercy from His people. God's response was mercy, sending manna, a kind of bread symbolic of Jesus. The bread of heaven sent from God to save (John 6:35). God's people were not satisfied for long with the manna, and they griped again—not only did they gripe, but they did not follow God's instructions (a test of obedience and trust in regard to the collection and storage of the manna (see Exodus 16). They grew weary of the manna and longed for more variety. God gave them what they longed for, sending a wind that drove quail in from the sea, a lot of quail. But the quail were not what was really needed, and before the quail were fully consumed, the Lord struck

His people with a plague because they had craved something other than His provision.

As our infants grow into childhood, they continue to want, don't they? It is the responsibility of their parents to discern the needs from the wants, and sometimes we, like God, give them what they ask for and let them bear the consequences because consequences are often life's best teachers.

When we mature as adults, we recognize that we have those childish sinful tendencies as well. The sinful nature within us wants what we do not have, and we are selfish children, discontent with our Father's provision. We might find victory in contentment over one circumstance in our lives, only to discover discontentment again when we are faced with a new challenge. God, forgive. God, have mercy. God, help us to trust and give us a spirit of contentment. May we learn from this revelation of You and Your care of Your people that griping where we are doesn't get us far.

Prayer: Lord, we pray that in Your power, we might be able to say with the apostle Paul as he states in Philippians 4 that we have learned the secret of being content in any and every situation, whether well-fed or hungry, whether living in plenty or in want, because we know that You will meet all our needs according to Your glorious riches in Christ Jesus. To our God and Father be glory forever and ever. Amen.

Summer Kayak

The turtles are sunning and so am I
As I watch the flit of a dragonfly
A large blue heron is fishing near shore
I am warm and full—couldn't ask for more
The splash of a fish…a bird takes wing
I stop to hear all nature sing
Summer's chorus, summer's song
Heard in my kayak as I drift along

A Lens to Keep Focused

I wish I could see clearly without my glasses, but, alas, the details of life become distorted without them. As time passes, this is becoming increasingly true for me. I waste too much time and effort trying to read and see what I am doing without the clarity that I need. "Why don't you just wear your glasses all the time?" you might ask. I'm vain. I guess I am a little prideful. Also, I forget to keep them with me so that I have them when I need them. I want to be a person who doesn't have to rely on something outside of myself to function, to see my environment, to see the world clearly. But I'm not that person. Nobody is that person, really.

The apostle Paul in Philippians 4:4–9 informs Christians that to see and experience God's peace, we need a lens to look through, and that lens is rejoicing in the Lord. Rejoicing in the Lord will help us focus to see and meditate on what is right, pure, lovely, admirable, excellent, and praiseworthy, and to practice those things. You see, He is the Creator of all that is good. When we focus on these things that are born from His goodness, peace comes. We see a godly perspective instead of a worldly perspective. That peace has the power to dispel anxiety over whatever is not from God—that which we can see that is not of God and that which we cannot see that we may be having trouble trusting God with. That peace has the power to guard our minds. That peace has the power to guard our hearts. It's not nearly so hard to see if we keep our glasses on.

Prayer:

> Be Thou my Vision, O Lord of my heart
> Naught be all else to me, save that Thou art
> Thou my best Thought, by day or by night
> Waking or sleeping, Thy presence my light.
> ("Be Thou My Vision," Audrey Assad,
> Conexion Media Group, Inc.)
> Amen.

The Gift

I have a story I want to tell
About a gift I love so well.
I have had the gift for quite a while,
But it's not old or out of style.
No other gift could ever compare;
My gift is special, priceless, and rare.
What type of gift could evoke such glee
From an insignificant me?
Was it something I did, something said?
Was it some great cause I have led?
What I've come to know and hope all learn,
My gift is not something you can earn.
In love it was given, faith secured,
The true being of God's own Word.
Jesus is the gift to me given,
Love, joy, peace, a life in heaven.

Treasure

(MATTHEW 13:44–46)

What do you treasure? A treasure, according to the *Merriam-Webster Dictionary* and the Thesaurus.com, is something you hold dear, cherish, and consider valuable or important. You esteem it. It is special. Matthew 6:21 says, "For where your treasure is, there your heart will be also." In Matthew 13:44–46, Jesus tells a parable about the kingdom of heaven, and it is compared to a treasure. When found, the man who found it was willing to give up all to possess the treasure. Why? Because what he was going to get was of much greater value than what he had.

The kingdom of heaven is where Jesus Christ is ruler and Lord. Have you found it? How valuable is it to you? Are you willing to join the kingdom of believers? Are you willing to place yourself in subjectivity to the Lord of the kingdom? Will you trust Him with your finances, your vocation, your relationships, and your leisure activity? Will you trust He knows better than you what you need? The kingdom of heaven starts in the heart of the individual, and when it grows, the world benefits eternally from the light it glows, the fruit it grows, and the Savior it knows. If your treasure is in a temporal kingdom, the kingdom benefits will be temporal as well.

Sometimes we are like the child who is unwilling to trade five pennies for four quarters. The child knows what he knows that five is more than four, but he does not know what he does not know—the *value* of the coins, the *worth* of the treasure. Are you willing to risk what you know—what you see and feel and touch—for what is unseen, spiritual, and eternal? Do you trust the King?

Prayer: Let this be our motto as citizens of the kingdom of our Savior, the Lord Jesus Christ: "For we live by faith, not by sight" (2 Corinthians 5:7). Lord, help us to live by faith and not by sight, as we can only do this in your strength. Amen.

Summer Friend

Under the tree is where the welcome's found. It's
where friends and neighbors gather 'round.
Flowers, birds, and squirrels are a sure delight.
The wind chimes, too, call out their invite.
Hospitality under this old tree
Is unlike any you'll ever see.
Swinging and chatting in a carefree way in the beginning or end of day.
This widowed neighbor, loved by young and old,
Each sharing their lives as they enfold.
She is never one to gossip or judge;
She finds the good in each one of us.
Inspiring us with care and concern,
A teacher to all who stop and learn.
Saddened to think thoughts of summertime's end,
when we all will miss our special friend.

Boast About This!

It's tempting to boast. People boast about all kinds of things—their accomplishments, accomplishments of relatives, personal experiences, educational achievements, things they have seen, places they have been, people they know, charitable giving, good deeds, hobbies, and even how many hot dogs or pies they can eat in one sitting. We all want some sort of validation, acknowledgment, appreciation—something to set us apart. We want to be special. Here is the great news: we *are* special. We are made in God's image, and when we know and trust Him, He can use us in a very special way! The problem with us is that our all-about-me tendencies want to take the credit. Acts 17:28 states that it is in Him (God) that we live and move and have our being. In 1 Corinthians 1:26–31, Paul reminds the church in Corinth (and us) that by human standards, most of us are not all that wise; but God in His wisdom chooses what the world thinks is foolish, lowly, and weak—not humanly wise, influential, or noble—to shame the worldly wise and strong. He chose the things not seen to nullify the things that are seen so that no one may boast before Him. This scripture reminds us that our righteousness, holiness, and redemption are ours because of God's gift to us in Christ Jesus. *Therefore*, "Let him who boasts boast in the Lord."

God's love in creating us and God's love in redeeming us through the sacrifice of Christ Jesus show us how valuable we are. But it is His kindness, His justice, His righteousness, His holiness, and His redemption at work in us that is evidence of greatness—and that greatness is His! First John 3:1 states, "How great is the love the Father has lavished on us that we should be called children of God! And that is what we are!" How special is that?

Prayer: God, forgive us for trying to steal Your glory. You have said in Jeremiah 9:23 and 24, "Let not the wise boast of his wisdom or the strong man boast of his strength, or the rich man boast of his riches, but let him who boasts boast about this: that he understands and knows me, that I am the Lord, who exercises kindness, justice and righteousness on earth, for in these I delight." Oh, that we would be your instruments in exercising these attributes of Yours and, in humility, give you all the glory for letting us be part of Your plan and for letting us be Your image bearers—for letting us know You. Show us Your glory! May we know You better so we can better do Your will and so we can better reflect Your glory. Amen.

Prayer for Our Young

Growing in inches, in wisdom, in spurts,
We watch with joy, but just a little, it hurts.
Blossoming in beauty, building in strength,
Moving along in life's time length.
Like a flower's bud on the verge of bloom,
This potential now we try to groom.
We pray all gifts will be used for good.
Your kingdom built, Lord, if You would.
May this growth be spread to all around;
May Your love and grace in them abound.

Like a Tree

(JEREMIAH 17:8; PSALM 1)

I love trees. There are no two the same. They all branch out differently. They are objects of beauty to me in all seasons. The green of a leaf is such a peaceful color, symbolic of life and of hope. Trees are not only beautiful but also functional. They provide shade and food and shelter for people, animals, and insects. They are strong, and they grow toward the light, making their way toward the skies. They sometimes make many bends and turns to find the way. I have heard that the roots of a tree, which are unseen, can occupy three times more space than the branches, which are seen. These unseen roots provide stability in times of adversity. One singular tree can be magnificent, and a group of trees can be spectacular. A group of the same types of trees, such as the pine or aspen, in the mountains are an awesome sight, and a forest with a plethora of tree varieties is a feast for the eyes of tree admirers. When their life is over, they continue to provide and are used for furniture, fuel, and paper products. They also leave behind nutrients for younger life and life yet to be born.

God created the tree. What a tribute to His majesty and power. Man, the crown of God's creation, is compared to a tree in Jeremiah 17:8. Listen to this comparison: "But blessed is the man who trusts in the Lord, whose confidence is in him. He will be like a tree planted by the water that sends out its roots by the stream. It does not fear when heat comes; its leaves are always green. It has no worries in a year of drought and never fails to bear fruit." Psalm 1 states that the man who does not walk the way of sinners but delights in God's law is like a fruitful tree whose leaf does not wither and who prospers in what he does.

I want to be like that fruitful tree! There is a song by Evie Karlsson called "Tree Song," perhaps inspired by this very verse. The lyrics are as follows: "I saw a tree by the riverside one day as I walked along, straight as an arrow and pointing to the sky, growing tall and strong. How do you grow so tall and strong? I said to the riverside tree. This is the song that my tree friend sang to me, 'I've got roots growing down to the water. I've got leaves growing up to the sunshine, and the fruit that I bear is a sign of life in me. I am shade from the hot summer sun-down. I am nest for the birds of the heaven. I'm becoming what the Lord of trees has meant me to be, a strong young tree.'"

Seedling, young tree, tree in the prime of life, or old tree—each is beautiful in its time. Each is called to a different type of fruitful life. Each one finding its way to the sun, or shall we say Son? This is the beauty of a tree, and the beauty of the one who trusts in the Lord.

Prayer: Let the beauty of Jesus be seen in me. Give me roots to hold on to the Word and reach for Jesus, the water of life. Give me a strong trunk from the wisdom derived from that Word to withstand the winds of trials and tribulations. Let the life of the Spirit be evidenced in my leaves and fruit, and may many be blessed because of my life. Like a tree, when others see me, may they see beyond me to the One who gives life. Amen.

Dysfunctional

Dysfunctional marriages, families, and friends,
We're all dysfunctional, from start to end.
Falling short of all we could possibly be,
Dysfunctional you, dysfunctional me.
Broken, defective, maladjusted, unfit,
In body and will, emotion and wit.
Thinking of how all this dysfunction could mend,
How to make straight this dysfunctional bend.
For this problem, there's one way we can go.
We all need God's grace, and we can't let go.
We can count on His power to fix our parts,
To change all our wills, and to cleanse our hearts.
He can give our dysfunction His added strength;
He takes our shortcomings and gives them length.
Revealing an us that is restored and whole,
An end to dysfunction in body and soul.

A Spiritual Lawn Inspection

(GENESIS 3:17–19)

> To Adam He said, "Because you listened to your wife and ate from the tree about which I commanded you, 'You must not eat of it,' cursed is the ground because of you; through painful toil you will eat of it all the days of your life. It will produce thorns and thistles for you, and you will eat the plants of the field. By the sweat of your brow you will eat your food until you return to the ground, since from it you were taken; for dust you are and to dust you will return."

Your lawn is cursed, you know. Of course, you know. You plant good grass seed, but the labor of planting isn't enough, is it? Untended, weeds will spring up. Crabgrass will choke out the good grass and rise above it. Before long, it's all you notice. In the spring, those dandelions may not look so bad—the yellow flowers even have a little bit of spring appeal. We all know, though, how ugly they become when the flowers are gone, sticking out like a stain on an otherwise clean shirt. They are counterfeits for real flowers; flowers whose beauty goes beyond the blossom!

Not only are there weeds, there is the mowing of the grass. Neglected grass is not conducive to the curb appeal of your home or to the appeal of your lawn-loving, lawn-tending neighbor. A lawn left to negligence affects—or shall we say defects—the whole neighborhood. Your weeds find their way into your neighbor's yard one way or another. It does not take long to see how weeds have a propensity to thrive. If we are not intentional about mowing, weeding, and replacing weeds with good seeds, our lawns are destined to become unsightly, unattractive, and destructive to the good seed that was initially sown in our lawn—and in our neighbor's lawn.

That's the curse that rests on our lawns. It's also the curse that rests on our spiritual lawns and the good seed that was planted in our hearts. We do not, however, have to resign to be overcome by the curse. That seed of truth has the power of life. If we protect it, and the conditions surrounding it, the weeds do not have to overcome, though they might pop up from time to time. We just have to deal with them when we see them! Once sown in us, that seed of truth can be reproduced and scattered throughout the world. And when the Spirit of God brings it to life, it is beautiful, attractive, and powerful. Like our lawns, it is a continual process of pulling out, trimming, tilling the hard ground, planting more good seed, and protecting it from elements and intruders. God, in His goodness, brings the life, the growth, and the beauty. He has made the curse conqueror available for our spiritual lawns. The ultimate combination weed and feed of God's Word: Christ's work and the ongoing transforming work of the Holy Spirit in us. It will be possible for God to see our lawns as perfect, and when you think about it, God deserves nothing less than a perfect lawn.

Prayer: "Let the beauty of Jesus be seen in me, All His wonderful passion and purity. O thou Spirit divine, all my nature refine, till the beauty of Jesus be seen in me" ("Let the Beauty of Jesus Be Seen in Me," Albert Orsborn) Amen.

Big Small Things

One summer day, as I mowed the grass,
Under a tree, I made a pass.
Above the noise of the motor's roar,
A song of jubilee did soar.
I paused to search out this singer's voice;
The lure of cheer prompting this choice.
I looked for the flashy, brilliant source
Of this bold and beautiful force.
And then I saw from where this song came—
A plain brown bird, an unknown name.
How she brightened that summer day
As she sang her song, so loud and gay.
I thanked God for the joy from small things,
Praying for boldness, His praise to sing.
For if God brings inspiration from a small bird on cue,
How much more can He encourage through me and through you?

Shine, Jesus, Shine

(MATTHEW 5:14–16)

In the summer, the days are longer. Strength and energy are often at their peak. The strength and energy that we find in Christ will often shine brightly during those years. Jesus said, "You are the light of the world. A city on a hill cannot be hidden. Neither do people light a lamp and put it under a bowl. Instead they put it on its stand, and it gives light to everyone in the house. In the same way, let your light shine before men, that they may see your good deeds and praise your Father in heaven" (Matthew 5:14–16).

There are many things in life that interfere with light being seen. Blindness, for example, would be an obstacle to see light. Clouds could obscure light. A dark place or a dark screen could block light. As Christians, we have been given a light, and we are told to let that light shine. In John 8:12, Jesus said, "I am the light of the world. Whoever follows me will never walk in darkness, but will have the light of life."

If we have Jesus, we have light to shine. Sometimes, if we are honest though, our reflection of His light do not shine very brightly. What are the obstacles blocking His light from being seen in you? Unconfessed sin? Pride? Lust? Depression? Despair? Fear? Selfishness? Ungratefulness? The list goes on, doesn't it? Sometimes the obstacles are of our own doing; sometimes they are not. Are we trying to shine on our own, forgetting to plug into the source, the true light—the light of the word, the light of the world? What do we need to do to remove the obstacles so that we can shine bright and pure and so that our good deeds can be seen and our Father in heaven is glorified? Have you asked God to move the obstacles that you cannot move or asked Him to help you shine His light so bright that it goes right through them?

We are called to shine. It is our purpose as children of light. What can you do to shine today?

Prayer: Jesus, You have broken the barriers of sin and death for us. Help us to break the barriers that are keeping us in darkness, Lord. Let the light of Your love shine through the darkness, into us, and through us. Be glorified through our lives. Shine, Jesus, shine!

Summer Bridge

When in summer's prime on productive track,
Often too busy to turn and look back.
Take special care that you don't fail to see
Distractions that pull you away from Me.
My truth in your heart is the bridge you need
To keep you from failing, to keep you free.

Autumn

Season of Reflection

Now autumn, arriving with dew on cool morning,
You come in the bounty and beauty of harvest.
Your countenance brings us happy and sad moments.
Your array of colors takes our breath away.
But you also usher in decay and coldness,
Leaving us aware of earthly mortality.
Your song is mellow; you bring reflection to thought.

"Help, I Can't See!"

When God calls us to follow Him, it sounds good in theory in the Sunday school lesson or small group discussion or in the pew at church. When His Spirit speaks to us and tells us to do what is perhaps unconventional, unprofitable, or uncomfortable, we are faced with that spiritual struggle: resist and play it safe or follow the Spirit. Once you have tested the Spirit and know that it is the true Spirit, which acknowledges that Jesus Christ has come in the flesh and that calls us to follow His example, then it is time to follow. I don't know about you, but my instinct is to cry out like a child alone in the dark, "But, God, I can't see where I am going!" That is true. I can't. You can't. We can't. The light of His Word illuminates just enough to see the path. It does not show everything along that path, and we can't see the destination until we get there. But we have our map. We have the Bible. We have His Word. We have Jesus, the One who went before us. We have promises—promises from a trustworthy God. Promises like "I will be with you" (Matthew 28:20), "I will help you" (Psalm 121:1–2), "I will give you what you need" (Philippians 4:19; Matthew 6:33), and "I will work it out for your good" (Romans 8:28). We have promises to hold on to.

So fix your eyes on what is unseen, as illogical as it may sound. Second Corinthians 4:18 states, "So we fix our eyes not on what is seen, but on what is unseen, since what is seen is temporary, but what is unseen is eternal." I'm not sure what that means for you right now.

Perhaps the call is to humility, and you have to leave behind some power or control. Perhaps that call is to a spirit of gratitude instead of negativity—to trust in His provision, whatever that looks like. Perhaps it is a call to change your vocation. Perhaps He is calling you to leave something that is distracting you from the good works He has called you to do. Is He calling you to take the path of forgiveness or reconciliation? Is He calling you to be His witness to love the unlovable?

We are Christians! We live by faith, not by sight! First Corinthians 3:189–19a3: 18–19a states, "Do not deceive yourselves. If any one of you thinks he is wise by the standards of this age, he should become a 'fool' so that he may become wise. For the wisdom of this world is foolishness in God's sight." Faith is not always logical. We are not meant to see the future. The future belongs to God. Trust Him with it.

Prayer: Help us, Lord, to just keep trusting You. Trusting and obeying—walking by faith and not by sight. Help us to do this simply, even when it's complicated. Help us to do it wholeheartedly, even when we are tempted to take a detour. Help us to do it always, for Your glory. Amen.

Listen to Grace

It is a problem that I can see—this dialogue going on inside of me.
Two voices that argue, attempts to persuade. I
try to discern with each case made.
One voice is coaxing; I'll call that one grace.
It tells me that I can still save face.
It steers me to thinking things aren't what they
seem; no matter the what, God can
redeem.
My value's not determined by what's achieved; it's more
about what I have believed. But the second voice only
wants to debate and relentlessly argues failure's fate.
"Whatever your goals, you will come up too
short—you're pathetic, pitiful" is its
retort.
"Just let opportunity pass right on by. Give in to defeat, don't even try.
Your best efforts will never, ever be good.
You're a failure, not misunderstood."
There's a bit of truth in the second voice heard—
or I'd disregard it as absurd.
Still I do realize which voice will devour and
which voice offers much-needed power.
I take a step forward, silencing this foe, and
ask grace alone with me to go.

Doubt

I'm ashamed to say I doubt sometimes. I know what James 1:6–8 says about doubt: "He who doubts is like a wave tossed about by the sea, blown and tossed about by the wind. That man should not think he will receive anything from the Lord. He is double minded and unstable in all he does."

So I pray for pure trust. I rationalize when I doubt that I am not doubting *God.* It's *me* I doubt. I doubt *my* decisions, *my* abilities, and the changes in my circumstances that I have chosen. What if I made the wrong choice? Well, thinking a little deeper, I guess I do doubt God. You see, I think my choice might work out badly, but I am forgetting that God works all things out for the good of those who love Him and are called according to His purpose (Romans 8:28). It doesn't make sense to us sometimes. All things, even a foolish decision? Even that. But, Lord, what about a selfish decision, a sin? Yes, even that, though there may be consequences that do not feel pleasant. God is bigger than consequences. So trust the One who is worthy of trust, but don't forget that even though you might be the one shooting the ball, God ultimately directs its course and decides when and if you score and the significance of that point within the context of the game. Perhaps it's the lessons you learn as you play the game that He is interested in, not whether you make the basket you were shooting at.

So what does this have to do with Isaiah 55? Well, sometimes we make choices where there is a less than tangible reward in sight in the eyes of the world. That's okay. Isaiah 55:2–3a tells us, "Why spend money on what is not bread, and labor on what does not satisfy? Listen, listen, to me and eat what is good, and your soul will delight in the richest of fare. Give ear and come to me; hear me that your soul may live." Also, verse 9–13 states, "As the heavens are higher than the earth, so are my ways higher than your ways and my thoughts than your thoughts. As the rain and snow come down from the heaven and do not return to it without watering the earth and making it bud and flourish, so that it yields seed for the sower and bread for the eater, so is my word that goes out from my mouth, it will not return to me empty, but will accomplish what I desire and achieve the purpose for which I sent it. You will go out in joy and be led forth in peace; the mountains and hills will burst into song before you, and all the trees of the field will clap their hands. Instead of the thorn bush will grow the pine tree, and instead of briers the myrtle will grow. This will be for the Lord's renown, for an everlasting sign which will not be destroyed."

So do it! Ask for wisdom, seek first His kingdom, and jump! God will catch you where you are and bring you to where He wants you to be.

Prayer: Sometimes we are so self-absorbed, we think it all depends on us. How grateful I am that it doesn't. Thank You for the reminder to spend ourselves on food for the soul, and You will accomplish the rest. Oh, and thank You for taking care of the failures—past, present, and future. Help us not to doubt that You are able to use us when we rely on Your power.

An Offering

I wanted to lift up an offering so all the world could see
I had a special light to shine inside of me.
I wanted to make a difference, to make right of all the wrong
To show I had answers for which others longed.
I tried so hard with all my might to lift my offering high,
Putting it down again with disappointment's sigh.
My offering looked unworthy and tainted. It was so unclean.
Effort's inadequacy was now clearly seen.
Then came to mind the offering that already had been made;
The shame of sin and failure on my Jesus laid.
So I take a different offering; it's all I have now to bring.
The precious name of Jesus, my Savior and King.

What If?

Have *you* ever played the what-if game? The scenarios of worry are as endless as the circumstances of life. What if I try and fail? What if I get hurt? What if I am embarrassed? What if somebody else has to help me? What if something bad happens to someone I care about?

Matthew 6:25–34 gives us these soothing words from our Savior: "Therefore I tell you, do not worry about your life, what you will eat or drink; or about your body, what you will wear. Is not life more important than food, and the body more important than clothes? Look at the birds of the air; they do not sow or reap or store away in barns, and yet your heavenly Father feeds them. Are you not much more valuable than they? Who of you by worrying can add a single hour to his life? And why do you worry about clothes? See how the lilies of the field grow. They do not labor or spin. Yet I tell you that not even Solomon in all his splendor was dressed like one of these. If that is how God clothes the grass of the field, which is here today and tomorrow is thrown into the fire, will he not much more clothe you, O you of little faith? So do not worry, saying, 'What shall we eat?' Or 'What shall we drink?' Or 'What shall we wear?' For the pagans run after all these things, and your heavenly Father knows that you need them. But seek first his kingdom and his righteousness, and all these things will be given to you as well. Therefore do not worry about tomorrow, for tomorrow will worry about itself.

Each day has enough trouble of its own." First Peter 5:7 tells us, "Cast all your anxiety on him because He cares for you."

Anxiety is fear, and where there is fear, faith cannot thrive. If we believe in a sovereign God who is in control over all things and who can and will work *all things* to our good if we belong to Him, then we have nothing to fear. We could never plan our lives better than God, who is able to give us "immeasurably more than we can ask or imagine" (see Ephesians 3:20).

So go ahead and play the what-if game, but don't forget the answer to the question when you ask it: There is no possible scenario that God is not in control of, and we know that our God is strong and our God is loving (Psalm 62:11–12a). Our God is more than able to take care of what concerns us today.

Prayer: Lord, in all circumstances, we know that we are more than conquerors through You, the One who loves us. Though sometimes our faith is found wanting, help us believe that neither death nor life, neither angels nor demons, neither the present nor the future, nor any powers either height or depth, nor anything else *in all creation* will be able to separate us from your love, God, the love that was made known to us through Christ Jesus our Lord. Amen and amen. (Taken from the words of Romans 8:37–39).

Who Am I?

There is too much of me or not enough.
You can fill me up or let me run out.
I can bind, and I can free.
I can make you hurry or slow down.
I am a gift, and I am a curse.
Nobody knows how much of me they will have,
Yet they will have had the same amount at the end of the day.
I am stolen, and I am given.
I am opportunity lost or gained.
I am cherished, and I am wasted.
You can track me or lose track of me
You can see evidence of my existence, but you cannot see me.
I bring joy, and I bring sadness.
You can control what you do with me, but you can't control me.
Who am I?

Faithful or Fearful?

(Matthew 25:14–28)

Jesus often taught his disciples in parables, and in Matthew 24 and 25, He uses some of these parables to describe what His coming again will be like. In this parable of the talents in Matthew 25:14–28, the distribution of the master's wealth was uneven. The master had every right to do what he wanted with what belonged to him. It was not for the servant to judge the master in regard to what was given him. The master was the distributor and the judge of those to whom he distributed. The parable informs us that the wealth was given according to the ability each servant had to manage it. It is notable that the master did not keep his treasure to himself; rather, he entrusted his valuables to his servants. Each servant had a designated amount to work with, a designated place to work, and a designated period of time known to the master in which to work.

At the end of the designated time, the man given the largest amount of wealth had doubled the wealth and brought it back to the master. The man with the moderate amount had also doubled the wealth and brought it back to the master. The master's expectations were met, and he promised a reward to those servants. There is no indication that he expected the servant with the moderate amount to produce the same as the servant who was given the largest amount to work with. Sadly, the man who had received the smallest amount became motivated by fear—fear of failure. He did not act in faith that what was given could be multiplied for his master. Not only did he fail to work with it, he hid it so it could not be seen or used. The master's expectations were not met. The servant had known better. In his heart, he knew that the master was able to multiply even in excess of the investment, but he failed to place his trust in what he knew to be true.

What has God given you to work with? Are you working hard, putting it to good use? Are you relying on faith that your Master knows your ability and has gifted you accordingly? Do not let fear or jealousy or discontentment or laziness be your master. Let love for your Master be your motivation. Trust that He has given you the right amount to work with and that He knows exactly what He is able to accomplish through you if you are a willing servant. Then live and act on faith.

Prayer: Please help us to be faithful with what we have been given. Let love, devotion, and respect for You, our Master, work in us and through us. Then, dear Lord, help us to believe in multiplication miracles! Amen.

Grace for Girls

Three little girls with pink-curler curls,
Sunday's best dresses tied with a bow,
In church pew they sit, all in a row.
Wash your face, live in grace,
Beyond yourself invest.
Weekly, a day of rest.
Three little misses, with hugs and kisses,
Shouting and tears with giggles and squeals—
The life that's between messes and meals.
Be polite, do what's right.
First see that chores are done,
Then go and have some fun.
Three whom we treasure, their growth we measure,
Watching to see if they will discern,
And the law of love begin to learn.
Please don't fight, shine your light;
Take each test, do your best.
Three women have grown now in their beauty.
They've taken the baton of duty.
Love husbands, children well,
God's grace ready to tell.
Show the way, remember, pray.
Seek the truth; in thanks, give.
This, the way, always live.

Respecting Boundaries

(PSALM 139:5–6)

> You hem me in—behind and before; you have laid your hand upon me. Such knowledge is too wonderful for me, too lofty for me to attain.

If you have parented children, you know how important it is to provide boundaries—boundaries that are dynamic, individualized, and set in place purposefully. Parents, being older and wiser than young children, have a responsibility to keep them safe and to determine what is best for them. Children, as you know, are not always in agreement with the boundaries that are put in place for them. Often they break the rules, and sometimes the lessons are painful. In time, as they grow, hopefully they become wiser and learn to trust their parents, gain respect for the boundaries that were set in place, and appreciate their love and concern. Sometimes that does not happen as soon as we parents would like! Sometimes we are also slow in learning to trust God.

God, as our heavenly Father, has also given us boundaries. I am not just talking about commandments about how to live, though those are definitely boundaries we will have consequences for if we do not respect them. I am also talking about what He permits to come into our lives or to not come into our lives. Perhaps you have unfulfilled longings or dreams, and perhaps there are restrictions placed on you outside of your control that are keeping you from realizing those dreams. As a parent must sometimes say no to their child who wants something that may not be what their parent thinks is best, so God at times places obstacles in our path that we may not understand. He does know what's best though, and our hearts are what He is interested in.

Have you come to a place in your relationship with God that you trust He has your best interest in mind, no matter what the obstacle? If we have had the benefit of loving parents, then we saw the sacrifices our parents made on our behalf, confirming they had our best interest in mind. When we see the sacrifice that God has made for us, we have no cause to doubt him either. Secure in His love, we can find contentment, whatever our lot.

Let us pray some of the words from Psalms as we reflect upon our boundaries: "Lord, You have assigned me my portion and my cup; you have made my lot secure, the boundary lines have fallen for me in pleasant places. Surely I have a delightful inheritance." Help me to trust You with all my heart and lean not on my own understanding. Amen.

A Thank-You Prayer

Thank You for Your work when my faith was small
When I doubted Your all-too-obvious call
Thank You for chiseling away at me
For it's through that pain I now feel free
Thank You for comfort when I was so frightened
For wisdom that led me to be enlightened
May this thankfulness now my faith renew
So that I am willing to follow You

Shapely Pots

Talk about a visual! This passage in Jeremiah provides us with a good one! Have you ever seen a potter working at the wheel? He starts with a wet, sloppy blob, and as the wheel spins and his hands gently touch the clay, something shapely begins to appear. The possibilities are endless. As the wheel spins and the potter's creation begins to change shape, he may decide to change its form or function. How ridiculous to think of the vessel objecting to the artist's design. As the wheels of time and circumstance spin, our Potter, our Father-God, may decide to change our shape as it seems best to Him. He made us, and we are His. He wants to change us when we are marred. He changes us as seems best to Him. Sometimes that means reducing us to a wet, sloppy blob again. A wet, sloppy blob of humility has a lot more potential for something beautiful that a marred vessel that resists or obstinately refuses reshaping. In Jeremiah 18, God is prophesying through Jeremiah toward his people, Israel, who were not looking like or living like the nation God had set them apart to be. Read verse 6, "'O house of Israel, can I not do with you as this potter does?' declares the Lord. 'Like clay in the hand of the potter, so are you in my hand, O House of Israel. If at any time I announce that a nation or kingdom is to be uprooted, torn down, and destroyed, and if that nation I warned repents of its evil, then I will relent and not inflict on it the disaster I had planned. And if at another time I announce that a nation or kingdom is to be built up and planted, and if it does evil in my sight and does not obey me, then I will reconsider the good I had intended to do for it.'" Talk about motivation!

God does what seems best to Him in regard to nations and in regard to His chosen children. He wants us to be compliant with His shaping so we can be used according to His purpose. He shapes and creates according to His Word and His will. How is God trying to shape you today, and are you willingly conforming to His design? Do not resist God as He shapes you to be a *perfect* vessel. John 1:1 states, "In the beginning was the Word, and the Word was with God and the Word was God." John 1:14 tells us, "The Word became flesh and made his dwelling among us. We have seen His glory, the glory of the One and Only, who came from the Father, full of grace and truth." But that's another story...or is it?

Prayer: "Change my heart, Oh God. Make it ever true. Change my heart, Oh God. I want to be like You" (taken from "Change My Heart, Oh God," by Eddie Espinosa).

Good Food

I would just love something good to eat
I'd love it much more if it was sweet
If it was something that came from you
I'd be grateful for the giver too
If you planned the meal with me in mind
I'd appreciate you were so kind
If you enjoyed my presence as we ate
I'd be much inclined to clean my plate
When the food is gone and I'd depart
You would be the one that blessed my heart

Just the Right Recipe

(ROMANS 8:9–21)

I don't know about you, but I love to cook. It is fun to put together just the right ingredients in just the right amount and come up with something that nourishes and blesses those who partake of it. My family and friends and I enjoy sharing these recipes—recipes that work to accomplish that goal of blessing and nourishing the ones we serve.

Once, as I was meditating on Romans 1:9–21, I thought, *Hmm...this is like a recipe from God! A recipe for life and a recipe for love!* Take note of what goes in and what stays out of this entrée. Here it is:

> Love must be sincere. Hate what is evil; cling to what is good. Be devoted to one another in brotherly love, Honor one another above yourselves. Never be lacking in zeal, but keep your spiritual fervor, serving the Lord. Be joyful in hope, patient in affliction, faithful in prayer. Share with God's people who are in need. Practice hospitality. Bless those who persecute you; bless and do not curse. Rejoice with those who rejoice; mourn with those who mourn. Live in harmony with one another. Do not be proud, but be willing to associate with people of low position. Do not be

conceited. Do not repay anyone evil for evil. Be careful to do what is right in the eyes of everybody. If it is possible, as far as it depends on you, live at peace with everyone. Do not take revenge, my friends, but leave room for God's wrath, for it is written: "It is mine to avenge; I will repay," says the Lord. On the contrary; "If your enemy is hungry, feed him; if he is thirsty, give him something to drink. In doing this you swill heap burning coals on his head." Do not be overcome by evil, but overcome evil with good.

I encourage you to try this recipe out. I know those around you will be blessed and nourished by this spiritual food!

Prayer: Lord, thank You for Your word! You have shown us how to live. We have tasted and seen that You are good. When we see the evil around us, help us to remember that with Your help, we can overcome evil with good. We give You thanks and praise because You, God, in Christ Jesus, have overcome evil with good. You bless us and nourish us through the broken body and shed blood of our Savior, Jesus Christ. May we go forward in gratitude and strength because of the spiritual food You provide. Amen.

A Mother's Prayer

Not mine, but Thine, oh Lord, I know,
But I still find it hard to let them go.
A path before them You have laid;
I, as a parent, my part now have played.
I wasn't given their path to see,
But to show them the way, then set them free.
I'm inclined to worry for what's in store.
I love them so; you love them more.
I now pray that as their lives will unfold,
They to Your promises will hold.
And when they each come to confess Your name,
Your children's lives will you reclaim.
Amen.

"Nothing Will Be Impossible for You"

(Matthew 17:14–27)

In this Bible passage, the words that Jesus said really jumped out at me: "Nothing will be impossible for you." The disciples of Jesus were deficient in the faith department. They were unable to heal the man's son from seizures he suffered from. "Why?" the disciples asked Jesus after He healed the son. "Why couldn't we drive it [the demon] out?" Jesus answered, "Because you have so little faith. I tell you the truth, if you have faith as small as a mustard seed, you can say to this mountain, 'move from here to there' and it will move. Nothing will be impossible for you." Wow! It was their lack of faith that interfered with God using them for the miracle. Where they failed, however, Jesus succeeded. Where we have failed, Jesus has succeeded.

Later in the same chapter, the tax collectors inquired about Jesus paying the temple tax (ironic as Jesus was the true temple, the dwelling of God, the Son of God—God with us). The sons of kings were evidently exempt from taxes, and so should Jesus be as the King of Kings, and so should the disciples be as members of the King's household of faith. Nevertheless, Jesus does pay the price for the taxes, and the exact amount is provided for both Peter and Jesus in the mouth of a fish! God's provision sometimes comes from a most unlikely source, doesn't it? Jesus made sure the cost required was covered. The disciples needed faith. We need faith, too, in the seemingly impossible situations of life. God is perfectly capable of any miracle, but what a concept that sometimes He accomplishes His purposes in and through His people, using their faith in Him and even using a fish, if that's the way he wants His plan to play out.

Prayer: I need it Lord, a little faith for those seemingly impossible hurdles in my life and the lives of those whose burdens I bear and bring to You. All powerful, perfect Provider, help me to trust that You are able to provide a miracle to accomplish what concerns me today and what concerns those I love. Help me to believe that You are able to do this and will do this according to Your perfect will. Amen.

Shoes

Barefoot, dirty, calloused running feet
Memories of childhood, free of care, so sweet
Saddle shoes are skipping off to start school
Sit quiet, listen, obey each rule
Gym shoes running, dribbling, basketball
Practice shooting, passing, hearing sport's loud call
Date and graduate, shoes with a heel
Test steps of adulthood, seeing how they feel
Love discovered, we light our candles
Time to walk the aisle in wedding sandals
Children's voices, playing many roles
Church shoes, slippers, flip-flops, wearing through the soles
In and out of patient rooms to give the needed care
Nurse shoes, once clean and white, showing now their wear
Thinking now and dreaming just what they might be
New shoes to discover, fitted just for me.

Reinstated

(JOHN 13:31–38; JOHN 18:15–18 AND 25–27; JOHN 21:15–22; MARK 16:20)

Scene 1, The Prediction (John 13:31–38): Jesus prophesies His physical departure and informs His disciples that they will not be following Him to His death and subsequent glorification at this time. He gives them a new command, which is not so new really, as it is embodied in the Ten Commandments given to Moses so long ago. Now they will have a new example to follow: "Love one another. As I have loved you, so you must love one another. By this all men will know that you are my disciples, if you love one another." Peter is stuck on the fact that he can't follow Jesus at this time and insists he would lay down his life for Jesus, but the perfect sacrifice was needed before the imperfect sacrifice could be acceptable. Jesus predicts that Peter will disown Him—not once, but three times. Our ability to follow the new command starts with knowing we can't do it on our own and loving and trusting the One who could and did; then we can follow in His sacrificial footsteps. As a Jesus follower, we know that His sufficient work is needed to make our work acceptable. Then, and only then, can we join Him in His kingdom work, loving one another and pointing them to Jesus.

Scene 2, The Prediction Fulfilled (John 18:15–18 and 25–27): Jesus is arrested, and under pressure, Peter denies his association with Jesus when he is interrogated. Peter did not want to identify with the sin and shame that accusers of Jesus were projecting on Him. Yet it was crucial for Peter to do that to be a useful servant. Like Peter, we have to admit that our identity without him is an identity that is unworthy of a holy God. Our identity with Him is perfect and empowering because through Him, our sin and shame have been crucified.

Scene 3, The Reinstatement (John 21:15–22): Peter was fishing again, his pre-Jesus occupation. Jesus appears for the third time since His death and resurrection and provides a miraculous fishing experience—one of the Bible's great fishing stories! When the disciples finished eating the fish that were caught, Jesus asked Peter if he loved Him more than these (the fish, the old occupation, the old way of life). Peter responds that he does, that Jesus knows he does. Jesus wants him to prove it: "Feed my lambs" (with the bread of life, the living water). Three times He asked, and three times Peter affirmed his love, but the repeated asking is painful—perhaps a reminder of his denial. The work of Jesus paved the way for Peter's work, but Peter's road to glorify God would not be an easy one. He hesitated for a moment, asking if it would be the same for John. Jesus told Peter that it was not his concern where John's path would take. Peter's path was between Peter and Jesus, just as my path and yours are between us and Jesus. Mark 16:20 states, "Then the disciples went out and preached everywhere, and the Lord worked with them and confirmed his word by the signs that accompanied it."

Prayer: You are so good, Lord, to those who love You, reinstating us in your service when we have failed You. Help us to trust that Your love in Christ was sufficient to make our love perfect. Confirm Your word in us by the signs that accompany it. For Your glory, amen.

Faith Prayer

(REVELATION 2 AND 3)

I wonder how your faith will be tested and tried?
Will it find its way out, what you have inside?
Will you remember first love, for which you worked hard?
In the hour of trial, your heart to guard?
Will you hold tight to faith when so little you own?
Will you be able to recall it's all a loan?
When darkness surrounds you, will you let it creep in?
Will you cry out to God to forgive your sin?
Will you stand up for truth when the others have strayed?
Will you trust that God keeps each promise He made?
Are your deeds complete? Were they all done for the Lord?
Or is it your glory you're trying to hoard?
Have you, in your stubborn pride, God's good grace ignored?
Did you trust Him to provide what you couldn't afford?
In word and deed, let there be no denial.
Keep them all, dear God, in their hour of trial.
Write your name on all their hearts, each door unlock;
May they open them wide when they hear Your knock
Help them to persevere in life's race as they run.
Give them a future vision to overcome,
A vision of Your presence, Your glory, Your throne.
A desire, above all, to be Yours alone.
I believe each of their hearts you are holding near.
I believe You are faithful, this prayer to hear.

Quilting Lessons

Colossians 3 shows us God's plan for us as Christians—His project, if you will. This project involves cutting the old things out of our lives that do not fall in line with the new thing that God is creating in and through us and allowing the characteristics of Christ to be woven through us, binding us together, one with another. This passage reminds me a little bit of a craft I enjoy—quilting. Quilts have always held attractiveness for me. They are homey, unique, functional, and beautiful. As I learned and began to practice the art of quilting, I realized there are some biblical principles in the craft that can be applied to my spiritual walk.

Lesson 1: Quilting starts with a plan. "Plan your work, and work your plan," the saying goes. You can follow examples of successful crafters who have gone before you or imagine your own design and its execution—but every plan has an end goal in mind. Jesus is a worthy goal.

Lesson 2: Success in life and quilting is not determined by working capital. You can create something beautiful with fabrics you already have. Do not fail to start because you don't have what you want. Trust that you have been given all you need. We have all we need in Jesus.

Lesson 3: Perseverance is not an option. A dream is not enough. With quilting and life, perseverance produces results. This means you might have to work through a bit of chaos before the scraps and pieces are arranged into something beautiful. When Jesus changes hearts, it is the beginning of the ongoing transformation of sanctification. Jesus perseveres in us as we follow Him.

Lesson 4: Take time to enjoy the process. In my quilting, I have opted to do it by hand, slowly and thoughtfully appreciating each stitch contributing to the grand design. Spending time with the Master Planner of my life develops my relationship with Him and my trust in Him. Time with Jesus is never wasted time.

Lesson 5: A perfect quilt is not attainable. Strive as we might, we will never achieve perfection, but strive we must because the work of striving confirms our faith. If we obsess about misaligned corners or imperfect stiches, we miss the big picture. As in life, God wants our best. Christ's perfection accomplishes the rest. Once the pieces of a quilt are arranged and sewed together, we see its beauty, and we notice that the strength, security, and warmth are found in its layers. God behind me, God before me, God with me—these are the layers of my life quilt, stitched with a thread of love and a prayer that God's purpose and glory will be achieved. In Jesus, we are perfect.

Prayer: Lord, thank You for giving me all I need from start to finish for my life quilt. You make everything beautiful in its time, and we cannot fathom what You do from beginning to end (Ecclesiastes 3:11). As You establish the work of Your hands, establish the work of our hands. May Your favor rest upon us (Psalm 90:17).

Mourning Dove

Oh, mourning dove with your sad, sad song.
For who, or for what, do you so long?
For days gone by or for days to come?
For tasks to do or ones undone?
When you mourn for all the things of earth,
do not forget you're of great worth.
Your Father in heaven sees from above
And cares for you out of His love.
Know that He's hearing your soulful cry and
sends His comfort from on high.
Wounds and worries, He's able to heal, so joy and gladness you will feel.

Comfort

(Isaiah 40)

Do you like comfort? I sure do. We all do, don't we? Comfortable clothes, comfortable foods, comfortable companions. The comfort of a mother's arms, a friend's kind words, the touch or embrace of a loved one. The comforts of life are a soothing balm to the hardships in a sinful and broken world, a sinful and broken self. There is no earthly comfort, though, that can compare to the comfort that comes from a heavenly Father's love. There is a favorite scripture that talks about comfort. Do you know it? Isaiah 40:1–2, a prophecy for God's chosen people: "Comfort, comfort my people, says your God. Speak tenderly to Jerusalem and proclaim to her that her hard service has been completed, that her sin has been paid for. That she has received from the Lord's hand double for all of her sins." Verse 6 states, "A voice says, 'Cry out,' and I said, 'What shall I cry? All men are like grass and all their glory is like the flowers of the field. The grass withers and the flowers fall because the breath of the Lord falls on them. Surely the people are grass. The grass withers and the flowers fall, but the Word of our God stands forever.'" Where is the comfort in that? It is in the very last line: "The Word of our God stands forever." Listen to the Word of our God that is found in John 3:16: "For God so loved the world that he gave his only begotten Son, that whoever believes in him shall not perish, but have eternal life." Do you hear it? Do you believe it? Are you comforted? I know I am! Let's close in prayer with the words of an old hymn.

Prayer: "Oh spread the tidings round, wherever man is found, wherever human hearts, and human woes abound. Let every Christian tongue proclaim the joyful sound, the Comforter has come. Lo, the great King of kings with healing in His wings, to every captive soul a full deliverance brings. And through the vacant cells, the song of triumph swells, the Comforter has come!" Thank You, Father, for the comfort with which You soothe our souls. Amen.

Is It You?

Is it You, Lord, the one that I see
When the waves are billowing over me?
Are You come to help the one You love? Will
you give me a sign from up above?
I know that my faith is very small; I so fear for my life if I should fall.
Will You save me, Lord, at your own cost
so that I will not be forever lost?
Yes, I am sure it's Your hand I see.
I see it is reaching out to touch me.
Jesus Christ, my Savior, strong to save; so
very willingly Your life You gave.

Supernatural Power

(Matthew 5:38–48)

Jesus said, "You have heard that it was said, 'Eye for eye, and tooth for tooth. But I tell you, do not resist an evil person. If someone strikes you on the right cheek, turn to him the other also. And if someone wants to sue you and take your tunic, let him have your cloak as well. If someone forces you to go one mile, go with him two miles. Give to the one who asks you, and do not turn away from the one who wants to borrow from you. You have heard that it was said, 'love your neighbor and hate your enemy.' But I tell you: Love your enemies and pray for those who persecute you, that you may be sons of your Father in heaven. He causes his sun to rise on the evil and the good, and sends rain on the righteous and the unrighteous. If you love those who love you, what reward will you get? Are not even the tax collectors doing that? And if you greet only your brothers, what are you doing more than others? Do not even pagans do that? Be perfect, therefore, as your heavenly Father is perfect."

These are the ones. The ones that I am prone to trip over. These are the words that cut my heart to see if it bleeds. These are the words that shine a light in the dark places of my soul. These are the words that reveal my need again for a savior. I am not perfect as my heavenly Father is perfect. My love is flawed. This kind of love that wants no revenge, that gives to the one who has evil intent—this love that brings enemies before the Father in prayer; this love that loves despite human inclination. This kind of love is supernatural. Do I believe God can give me supernatural power? Do you believe God can give you supernatural power? Lord, give us faith! Lord, give us your power!

Prayer: Father God, who created all mankind and demonstrated Your own love for us in this while we were still sinners, Christ died for us. Unite us with Christ, our perfection, and fill us with obedient and sacrificial love. Forgive us our debts as we forgive our debtors. Amen.

Autumn Hike

Leaf on leaf in multiple shades of brown rustle loudly underfoot
Meshing into one caramel-colored blanket, covering all the earth
Cool lake breezes, intermittent sun rays
Leak through branch artwork
Woven upward to meet them
Step by step, with multiple twists and turns
Separate yet together
Meshing into one long, winding journey
Covered all with Your grace
Heartfelt gratitude for long-lasting love
Leak through the tapestry of memories
Woven upward to meet Him

Divine Initiative, Human Action, Divine Response

(MATTHEW 9)

Faith—where does it come from? Ephesians 2:8 states, "For it is by grace you have been saved, through faith—and this not from yourselves, it is the gift of God—not by works, so that no one can boast. For we are God's workmanship, created in Christ Jesus to do good works, which God prepared in advance for us to do."

Romans 3:10b–11 states, "There is no one righteous, not even one; there is no one who understands, no one who seeks God."

On our own, we would not seek God, but He, in His grace, opens our spiritual eyes and ears to One knocking on the door of our hearts; and He wants us to act according to the faith we have received. Revelations 3:20 states, "Here I am! I stand at the door and knock. If any one hears my voice and opens the door, I will come in and eat with him, and he with me."

When we open the door, the divine response follows. In Matthew 9, there are several accounts of the grace and mercy of Jesus Christ toward those who were sick and suffering. These accounts of the paralytic, the woman subject to bleeding, the ruler with the daughter that had died, the two blind men, and the demon-possessed man are faith examples. We are told that either the one who was afflicted or the one who was interceding on the behalf of the afflicted responded to the Savior in an act of faith by word or deed, or both. When they did, the miracle took place.

Do you recognize your need? Do you hear Him knocking? Will you respond in word and deed to the spark of faith that He has ignited? Jesus can heal! Jesus will heal! Jesus can use you, and Jesus can use me to show His power. When it happens, it will be a miracle!

Prayer: Increase the faith of your people, Lord, to act in faith. We believe that You are faithful to provide the miracle we need. In Your time and in Your way.

| JOANN DEKKER

Autumn Bridge

When in the Autumn, changes you face
The inevitable coming of the end of the race
You may want to listen to the call of despair
But if you look in the distance, there's a bridge that is fair
Redemption is that bridge that I freely give
Trusting in its power, you'll go on in faith to live

Winter's come with vigor and strength, harsh, brisk, barren.
A change in dress, you require from all nature
Earth's colors fading to shades of gray and white
The rivers cease their flow in your icy cold stare
My appearance changes too, in preparation
Quietly we both anticipate our triumph
You sing a song of promise and hope to hearts

(MATTHEW 25:1–13)

O il—it's a resource that provides opportunity to give light to the lamp holder; it's the fuel to keep a fire going. Fuel, of course, must be burned up; it must be used up to keep light available. There is more for the taking, but deliberation is required to have that oil, to keep that oil. Sacrifices must be made to find it: "You will seek me and find me when you seek me with all your heart" (Jeremiah 29:13). There are sacrifices of time: "Come near to God and he will come near to you" (James 4:8a). Sacrifices of money may be required: "Go, sell everything you have and give to the poor, and you will have treasure in heaven. Then come, follow me" (Mark 10:21b). There will also be sacrifices of self-will: "Then Jesus said to his disciples, 'If anyone would come after me, he must deny himself and take up his cross and follow me'" (Matthew 16:24). Fill my cup, Lord. Fuel my lamp. Prompt me to go to you to keep my oil supply abundant.

Blessed is the one who knows the oil is precious enough to make a sacrifice for it. Not just once for the initial supply, but daily, like food, to keep us functioning. The oil provides the sustenance we need for the waiting, for the crisis, for each moment. Yes, God will give us oil when we ask humbly and when we know that He is the only source—His Word, His presence, His sacrifice—to make it available to us. One person's supply is insufficient for two people. Get your own oil so you can see the bridegroom yourself—the Savior with His tender love, His amazing grace, His power, His might, and

His unfathomable glory. Do not be spiritually lazy. Do not be unprepared. Do not miss the banquet that has been prepared. Do not be left in darkness.

Prayer: "Give me oil in my lamp, keep me burning. Give me oil in my lamp, I pray. Give me oil in my lamp, keep me burning. Keep me burning 'till the break of day" (Hymn author unknown, CRG).

W eak, unwell, decrepit, and old,
Many are the stories that they have told.
Sometimes told again and again,
Memory, you see, has been lost to them.
Eyes dull and dry with reddened rim,
Sight's enlightenment has now grown so dim.
Their face masked with an empty gaze,
Visions appearing behind all the haze.
Raise your voice and speak out real loud,
Best to forget it if they're in a crowd.
Trapped in a world that is their own,
Hearing those voices that they have once known.
Skin so fragile, easily torn,
Painted with bruises that now must be worn.
Feet are swollen to twice the size,
Bringing them such pain on attempt to rise.
Inability to stand tall,
Fighting to hold on to dignity's call.
Struggling at times to even breathe,
Permission ungranted to take their leave.
Thoughts of their care rest in my mind;
A special compassion, they helped me find.
Souls to nurture wounds to attend,
But gracious gifts until life's end.

(Ecclesiastes 12)

"Remember your Creator in the days of your youth, before the days of trouble come, and the years approach when you will say, 'I find no pleasure in them'" (Ecclesiastes 12:1). The teacher in this passage goes on to make very creative, poetic analogies to the process of aging, when pleasure diminishes along with eyesight and strength. The clouds that return after the rain sound like a reference to depression, a sadness that persists, even after the tears are gone. The grinders—teeth—are few and cease to function. The voice grows weak, and sleep is elusive in the morning hours. The golden bowl is broken, the pitcher shattered, the wheel broken at the well—perhaps referring to the loss of the function of elimination. There is fearfulness of falling and dangers. Do you find these words dismal and hopeless? God forbid that we should be without hope. We are not without hope, and we do not only have future hope, but we have hope in the present. We have opportunity in this day of life, and we are advised in this passage not to let it pass us by. Remembering that we are dust, we are urged to seize the opportunity to look to our Creator, God, the one who formed us, the One who pitied our helpless state and provided the way through the sacrifice of Christ Jesus for us to have eternal life. Yes, the One who provided the way for our spirit to go on living after our body dies! Let's acknowledge our Creator, Savior, and Redeemer while we can—while we have life and breath here and now in this designated window of opportunity. Whether we are five or ninety-five, we are not promised tomorrow, but we are promised salvation today when we bring our sin and helplessness to Christ Jesus, accepting Him as Savior and Lord. Revelation 22:17 says, "The Spirit and the bride [which is the church] say, 'Come!' And let him who hears say, 'Come!' Whoever is thirsty, let him come; and whoever wishes, let him take the free gift of the water of life."

Prayer: Oh Lord, we thank You for the gift of life today. We acknowledge that many opportunities to love You and serve You with all our hearts have been lost. Give us a repentant heart for this. Today is a call to restore relationship with You and accept Your gift of salvation in Christ Jesus. Today is a new day to bring a message of hope for the hopeless, peace for the troubled, rest for the weary, and life for the dying. Holy Spirit, quicken the hearts of those that have not yet responded to Your call to come and quicken the hearts of those who have responded to come closer and share the hope they have. The time is now. Amen.

Millions of sparkling snow diamonds
Glimmering across snow-covered field and pond
A brisk wind is felt on my cold face
World so white, intense, bright, silent
The wonder of tranquility overwhelms
A wet tear is felt on my cold face
Pondering footprints left behind
I hesitate, reluctant to disturb the pristine pureness before me
Apprehension lines my cold face
The ominous cry of a crow pierces the stillness
A final spurring to forward motion, leaving behind still more footprints
A warm sun is felt on my cold face

(ISAIAH 40:21–31)

I have become a bit fascinated with eagles recently, as we have been spotting them at our lake cabin and also in the park by our Indiana home. Watching them fly is a beautiful sight. Looking at online video footage, eagles can be seen attacking animals three times their size. Eagles are strong, and they also have incredible eyesight. According to Wikipedia and an article by Anthony Bouchard (November 6, 2018), the eyesight of eagles can be eight times that of human beings.

Isaiah 40 mentions eagles and provides us with a visual that speaks to the strength God is able to provide to the tired and weary so they are able to soar on wings like eagles. With a seven- to nine-foot wingspan, eagles do indeed soar with what seems like very little effort. Like an eagle, when we are lifted above the obstacles that loom large on the ground, our new perspective helps us see the bigger scheme of things. In that perspective, strength is regained and hope is invigorated like unto the strength and hope of youth, even surpassing that kind of strength and hope. This is the sustaining strength of the God who calls the stars by name. Do not complain that your way is hidden from the Lord or that your cause is disregarded by your God. His eyesight is keener, His strength is greater, and His perspective is above the circle of the earth. He is able to help you fly like an eagle!

Prayer: Lord, "When I am down, and oh, my soul, so weary. When troubles come, and my heart burdened be. Then, I am still and wait here in the silence, until you come and sit awhile with me. You raise me up, so I can stand on mountains. You raise me up to walk on stormy seas. I am strong when I am on your shoulders. You raise me up to more than I can be" (lyrics from a song by Josh Groban).

F reedom's call against communist rule,
Denial of inalienable rights, the fuel.
Ideology now being put to test
As family relationships show unrest.
Planning escape in the dark of the night,
Through barbwire fence, he made his flight.
Surrounded by dogs, to prison taken,
Nearly starved, but hope unshaken.
Then to home he did return.
Inspired, a better plan to learn.
Swimming and working to make body strong;
Resolute, determined to leave political wrong.
The Danube River was now the route;
Three in one hundred would make their way out.
A grueling swim, then more obstacles to face
Before the outcome is seen to this incredible race.
When exhausted, weak, cold, and wet,
A wall of rock at river's edge was met.
Then was given a possibility to see
A cleft in that rock caused by a tree.
To this branch of hope he clung for a time;
With dawn's near approach came a treacherous climb.
This ending in capture—to a refugee camp sent,
Still holding to hope while this time was spent.
Granted permission, America to go,
Welcomed by Christians, whose love would show.
Claiming their God as his own Lord,

Adding a wife and two sons, adored.
As an American citizen, he now has his place;
To the plight of a refugee, he gives a face.
His were lessons in courage—how to be brave,
Learning in the process that God will save.
Working hard, a family raised well,
He knows he has a story to tell.
His story he says is not really his;
It's God's story in him that is what lives.
God's overwhelming story of grace
Is what brought him to this time and place.
In America, he found freedom to choose;
In Christ, a life he cannot loose.
Freedom's meaning to him now is clear,
Risking life for what you hold most dear.
If in God's grace we are given to see
We all are refugees wanting to flee.
The power of sin, our freedom's foe;
The rock of ages protects our soul.
To the branch of life we tightly cling,
Assuring salvation through faith to bring

(Exodus 33)

In this passage of the account of God's deliverance of His people from slavery, God responds favorably to Moses's request and assures him that His presence would go with him and the Israelites to the promised land. Moses then asks God to show him this presence—His glory. "Then the Lord said, 'There is a place near me where you may stand on a rock. When my glory passes by, I will put you in a cleft in the rock, and cover you there with my hand until I have passed by. Then I will remove my hand and you will see my back; but my face must not be seen.'"

God knew that Moses could not stand in His presence. He could not see His face and live. Even though God had expressed that He was pleased with Moses and He knew him by name, Moses was still a sinful man, and a sinful man could not endure the presence of a perfect and holy God. So God provided a rock for his safety.

When I think of a rock, I think of strength and security. In 1 Corinthians 10:1–4, the symbolism of the rock is revealed: "For I do not want you to be ignorant of the fact, brothers, that our forefathers were all under the cloud and that they all passed through the sea. They were all baptized into Moses in the cloud and in the sea. They all ate the same spiritual food and drank the same spiritual drink; for they drank from the spiritual rock that accompanied them, and that rock was Christ."

Jesus, our rock, gives us the strength and security to come to God because we stand on His perfection and holiness. Fanny Crosby, the American poet, saw that rock. Though she was blind, she saw clearly with spiritual eyes. It is my prayer that God will open our spiritual eyes to the rock of our salvation. A stumbling stone to the one who does not believe in His strength and power, but a haven of love and protection for those who hold fast to the rock for protection, security, and strength.

Let's close in prayer with Fanny's beautiful hymn "He Hideth My Soul."

> Prayer: "A wonderful Savior is Jesus my Lord, a wonderful Savior to me; He hideth my soul in the cleft of the rock, where rivers of pleasure I see. A wonderful Savior is Jesus my Lord—He taketh my burden away; He holdeth me up and I shall not be moved; He giveth me strength as my day. With numberless blessings each moment He crowns, and, filled with His fullness divine, I sing in my rapture, "O Glory to God for such a Redeemer as mine! When clothed in His brightness transported I rise to meet Him in clouds of the sky; His perfect salvation, His wonderful Love, I'll shout with the millions on high. He hideth my soul in the cleft of the rock that shadows a dry, thirsty land; He hideth my life in the depths of His love, and covers me there with His hand, and covers me there with His hand." Amen.

There is a moment etched in time
Within the recesses of my mind.
We gazed out the window, my Mom and I,
At one lone leaf on a branch up high.
My mother was restless, her days but few;
She seemed to think she had something to do,
Some place to go, but she did not know where;
I bade her be still and stay in her chair.
Nourishment for life was no longer found;
Before November's end, she was laid in the ground.
Like the lingering leaf, she was soon let go
To be covered in a blanket of snow.
If this were the end, how could I cope?
So I fix my eyes on the branch of hope,
For soon I know that I will see
A bud of new life stemming from that tree.
So lingering leaf, it's okay to fly,
For I know you belong to the One Most High,
Who reveals to us if we have faith to see
That life is meant for eternity.

(PSALM 143)

My mother died in our home. She always loved listening to Christian music, and my son-in-law had given me a CD on which words from Scripture were put to music. I played that CD over and over, more than all the others CDs we had. It was quiet and soothing. When Psalm 143 was sung, it seemed to be her spirit crying out to God. That psalm has been special to me ever since her death. It reminds me of her faith, of my faith, of God's faithfulness to the very end when He is all there is to cling to. He is all we have to cling to anyway that makes a real difference in life, but this sure becomes evident when mind and body fail; when we are packing up the few meager belongings left, knowing there is no need for any of it—for the spirit alone lives on—for now. When a spirit departs from the body and is separated from the flesh, the last enemy is silenced for the soul that is hidden in the unfailing love of the Lord. Then, as we lay the body to rest, the hands that held and served, the smile that said we were special, the voice that spoke truth and sang praise, and the heart that loved, we call to mind the resurrection of our Christ and the promised resurrection of all who die in Him. The body that is sown is perishable, it is raised imperishable (1 Corinthians 15:42), and the great deceiver and all whose names are not written in the book of life will be subject to a second eternal death (see Revelations 20:7–15). I know my mother is with the Lord she loved. I know when I pass from death, it will be to life. What about you?

Prayer: "O Lord, hear my prayer, listen to my cry for mercy; in your faithfulness and righteousness come to my relief. Do not bring your servant into judgment, for no one living is righteous before you. The enemy pursues me, he crushes me to the ground; he makes me dwell in darkness like those long dead. So my spirit grows faint within me; my heart within me is dismayed. I remember the days of long ago; I meditate on all your works and consider what your hands have done. I spread out my hands to you; my soul thirsts for you like a parched land. Answer me quickly, O Lord; my spirit fails. Do not hide your face from me or I will be like those who go down to the pit. Let the morning bring me word of your unfailing love, for I have put my trust in you. Show me the way I should go, for to you I lift up my soul. Rescue me from my enemies, O Lord, for I hide myself in you. Teach me to do your will, for you are my God; may your good Spirit lead me on level ground. For your name's sake O Lord, preserve my life; in your righteousness, bring me out of trouble. In your unfailing love, silence my enemies; destroy all my foes, for I am your servant" (Psalm 143). Amen.

I'm dreaming of a white Christmas
The world is just as it should be
Decked with glowing lights
Red colors, bright
Piercing the darkness in the night
I'm dreaming of a white Christmas
There is a tree forever green
And love's beauty glistens
As all men listen
To truth's song ringing in their ears
I'm dreaming of a white Christmas
A table set with choicest foods
Each loved one is present
I hear words resounding
"God's love is pure, and He is good"
I'm dreaming of a white Christmas
I hear the carols that we sing
And through the music's beauty
We claim Christ is worthy
To reign forever as our King!

(Luke 2)

> But the angel said to them, "Do not be afraid, I bring you good news of great joy that will be for all people."

Our grandson was the angel in the preschool Christmas program, chosen to announce to the shepherds that the Messiah had come. My daughter practiced his lines with him, and he was ready on the day of the event. When his moment came, he hesitated—a few brief seconds of trepidation, perhaps, as he searched for the words. You could almost see him thinking, and then his face lit up and the words came to him—at least the gist of the words came to him. With bold and confident enthusiasm, he proclaimed, "I got good news!"

I realized I had been holding my breath. I exhaled in relief and smiled. He remembered. He knew what he needed to know. He had the courage to tell it. He believed and remembered. He had good news to tell; the grammar could wait.

He is almost sixteen now, our beautiful boy. Sometimes when I pray for him, I find myself holding my breath. When he is put on the spot, no matter what the challenge, will he remember he's got good news? It's news of great joy for all people and for him, personally. Then, as I am praying, I call to mind God's faithfulness. I exhale in relief as I close my prayer, trusting the faithful One to remind him about the good news at just the right time and in just the right place.

Jesus has come; there is grace. Jesus has come; there is hope. Jesus has come; there is joy. Jesus has come; there is peace. Jesus has come; He has shown us how to love, how to be courageous, and how to trust the Father's will.

Prayer: "May God himself, the God of peace, sanctify you through and through. May your whole spirit, soul and body be kept blameless at the coming of our Lord Jesus Christ. The one who calls you is faithful and He will do it" (1 Thessalonians 5:23–24). Amen.

W ell, I know that there's a God above,
And I heard that He's a God of love.
He knew my name before my life began.
He made the sun, the moon, the sky,
The oceans deep, and the mountains high.
And all creation sounds His Hallelujah.
Then I heard about God's Son who came;
He healed the blind, the sick, the lame.
I heard He is the Way, the Truth, the Life.
He died, His broken child to save;
He rose to life up from the grave.
He lives now to receive our hallelujahs.
Now I have the Spirit that was given,
The Comforter that's come from heaven.
To help me speak God's truth and show His way.
He gives me hope, He gives me love,
He brings me peace from up above;
A light to shine, a voice of Hallelujahs.
Someday I'll take my final breath;
I'll pass to life from this world's death.
I'll see my Lord and Savior face-to-face.
For in God's Son, the work was done;
His love and grace, the victory won.
And I'll live on to sing His hallelujahs.

(Hymn by Stuart K. Hine, 1 Chronicles 29:10b–12)

Most Christians are familiar with the hymn written by Stuart K. Hine, "How Great Thou Art." It's my life's song. When I was a child and my eyes were opened to the awesome wonder of the world, my heart was touched, and I knew there was a God. "When I in awesome wonder consider all the worlds thy hands have made." I knew He created and was sustaining the world, from the mountain's grandeur to the birds singing sweetly in the trees to me—to my need of Him and His provision for that need in so many ways. Yes, I remember lying on my back in an open field and looking up at the sky and being touched by His presence. As a young adult, I also remember falling, rebelling, and knowing He was the only one who could pick me up; and "I could scarce take it in—that on the cross, my burden gladly bearing, He bled and died to take away my sin!" It was personal. The final verse of this song is the climax of the salvation story when we will see the glory of the Lord revealed and be taken to our eternal home where the dwelling of God is with man, with His church, with me, where joy is complete and the greatness of God is fully realized. What I know of God's greatness causes my heart to swell, and I know only in part. What I will know is an ecstasy yet to be realized. Has your soul sung of His greatness lately?

Prayer: "Praise be to you, O Lord, God of our father Israel, from everlasting to everlasting. yours, O Lord, is the greatness and the power and the glory and the majesty and the splendor, for everything in heaven and earth is yours. Yours, O Lord, is the kingdom; you are exalted as head over all. Wealth and honor come from you; you are the ruler of all things. In your hands are strength and power to exalt and give strength to all. Now, our God, we give you thanks, and praise your glorious name" (David's Prayer, 1 Chronicles 29:10b–13). Amen.

In eastern sky, creeping forward, stealing the grip of darkness
Clothed in rosy pink
A newborn life, bursting from womb's oblivion
Morning's dawn of hope
In fullest strength, pushing forward with purpose and resolve
Journey's momentum peaking
A wind-driven wave, rushing toward shore's destiny
Noon's march of hope
Anticipation realized, breaking force to shoreline
Hope ebbs into reality
Weariness melds into diminishing vision, excepting that of a western sky
Evening's painting of hope
With subtlety arriving, clothed in a gown of ebony
Sprinkled with diamonds
The jewels of promise illuminated
Nighttime's rest of hope

It is sometimes the longing prior to an expected event that heightens the joy. Anticipation often accentuates excitement. Longing may heighten our anticipation for what God promises us, but the joy that is yet to be realized we can now only imagine. What will it be like to experience the fullness of the presence of God in a world that is new and free of the curse of sin?

There are differing points of view about the interpretation of biblical prophesies on what the end times and heaven will be like. I am okay with not being so clear on the particulars. This passage is the one that I hold on to. The picture it paints heightens my anticipation. I know it is all I could ever want and all I could ever need, but it's beyond my imagination. It is a promise worth living for and worth dying for. How can we, who have tasted the goodness of God that contrasts the bitterness of what this broken world offers, long for anything else? Listen to the apostle John's account according to the vision he received and recorded in the book of Revelation 21:1–5a. This is the realization of your hope; you who are children of God and heirs of this holy city. Envision the glory of the Lord your God and the place He has prepared for you. Eagerly expect that it will be infinitely more than what you could possibly even hope for.

> Then I saw a new heaven and a new earth, for the
> first heaven and the first earth had passed away,

and there was no longer any sea. I saw the Holy City, the New Jerusalem, coming down out of heaven from God, prepared as a bride beautifully dressed for her husband. And I heard a loud voice from the throne saying, "Now the dwelling of God is with men, and he will live with them. They will be his people, and God himself will be with them and be their God. He will wipe every tear from their eyes. There will be no more death or mourning or crying or pain, for the old order of things has passed away." He who was seated on the throne said, "I am making everything new!" (Revelation 21:1–5a)

Prayer: "Hallelujah! For the Lord God Almighty reigns. Let us rejoice and be glad and give Him glory!" (Revelation 19:6b–7a). Amen and amen.

Come, thou long-expected Jesus; O come, O come, Emanuel
Once in royal David's City—O little town of Bethlehem
What child is this? Thou didst leave thy throne on high
Away in a manger
Hark, the herald angels sing, angels we have heard on high
Angels from the realms of glory; it came upon a midnight clear
While shepherds watched their flocks by night
The first Noel
Silent night, O holy night
My soul doth magnify the Lord, brightest and best of the sons
I know that my Redeemer liveth
Mary, did you know?
Good Christian men rejoice; oh come, all ye faithful
Ring the bells; go tell it on the mountain
Joy to the world, for unto us a child is born
All is well

(Romans 8)

If anyone ever asks you, "What is the Bible all about?" or "What do Christians believe?" I think Romans 8 is a very good summary. There is no condemnation for those who accept the sin offering of God's Son come to earth in the likeness of sinful man. Like us in the flesh, but unlike us in the spirit, for He lived in perfect obedience, doing what we could not. He paid our debt. Those who accept this sacrifice are saved and are controlled by the Spirit of God. The mind controlled by the Spirit of God has life and peace. The mind controlled by the Spirit of God is freed from the slavery of fear and sin and free to put to death the misdeeds of the body. Does that mean we do not suffer the effects of sin any longer? Does it mean we will stop sinning? No, not yet. We do suffer. We groan for the time when all creation will be liberated from its bondage to decay and brought to glorious freedom. We long for the glory that will be revealed in us, for our inheritance as God's children. Our flesh is still sinful, but our spirit is aligned with God, who empowers us. He alone can change our will to sin and our will to be our own God to a will that submits to Him for our good and for His glory. He alone can forgive us when we do sin so we can come into His presence clean and holy. Even in our sin and suffering, we rejoice because we know that we are more than conquerors in life, in death, in spiritual warfare, in the present, and in the future—all because of God's incredible love for us. There is nothing in all creation that can separate us from that love. That love that came to a virgin in the form of a baby boy. There is nothing that can separate us from the inheritance that is ours because of this King—the Son of God and Son of man, the death conqueror. There is nothing that can destroy the bridge that the person and work of this Jesus Christ gives to bring those who believe safely home.

Prayer: "All is well, all is well. Angels and men rejoice. For tonight darkness fell into the dawn of love's light. Sing ale, sing alleluia. All is well, all is well, let there be peace on earth. Christ's come, go and tell that He is in the manger, sing ale, sing alleluia. Born is now Emmanuel, born is our Lord and Savior. Sing alleluia, sing alleluia, all is well" ("All is Well" by Michael W. Smith). Thank You, Lord Jesus for Your perfect obedience, for Your perfect sacrifice, and for being the perfect manifestation of the Father's love. Thank You that we can say all is well with my soul.

It's quiet now, but I almost see
The faces in my memory.
These days, now past, brought us bonding joys,
Our love to each, our girls, our boys.
It's quiet now, but I almost hear
Voices of those I hold most dear.
These days, now past, brought relief from care,
From all our work's wear and tear.
It's quiet now, but I almost smell
The aromas we know so well.
These days, now past, these moments in time,
Are something I thank God were mine.
It's quiet now, but I almost touch
Your long hair that I love so much.
These days, now past, when I weaved your braid,
Held the wood carving that you made.
It's quiet now, but I almost taste
The nourishment that we once ate.
These days, now past, leaving me so filled,
Still satisfy me when I'm stilled.
It's quiet now, and as raindrops fall,
I won't let myself be sad, no not at all,
For in these days now past, God gave me
A glimpse into eternity.

(DEUTERONOMY 32; JOSHUA 3 AND 4)

Winter, a quiet season of life. A time of remembrance. A looking-back-at-life's-meaningful-moments. What makes moments meaningful? There's a catchphrase I hear from time to time, "It was a God thing." "God things" are the truly meaningful moments. The story of your life is a God thing. Moments of joy, faith-strengthening events, comfort and peace through trials, sin's consequences, and God's restoration—these are all meaningful moments that are revelations of truth and wisdom. Stop! Stop and let me tell you what the Lord has done for me. I will not forget to remember.

In the Old Testament, in the stories recorded in Deuteronomy 32 and Joshua 3 and 4, God did not want the Israelites to forget to remember what He had done for them. In Deuteronomy 32, Moses was about to die, but before he left, he sang a song, "Listen, oh heavens and I will speak; hear, O earth, the words of my mouth. Let my teaching fall like rain and my words descend like dew, like showers on new grass, like abundant rain on tender plants. I will proclaim the name of the Lord. Oh, praise the greatness of our God! He is the Rock, His works are perfect, and all His ways are just. A faithful God who does no wrong, upright and just is He." Moses then goes on to tell what God had done and prophesies the disaster that will come when Israel forgets to remember.

Moses dies. Joshua assumes leadership, and God once again displays His power and glory by stopping the flow of the Jordan River, heaping it up so that Israel could cross on dry ground.

Afterward, the Lord told Joshua to gather twelve stones to serve as a sign of what the Lord had done so that when their children asked, "What do these stones mean?" they could remember and tell what the Lord had done for them.

What about you? How many stones has God given you to lay as a memorial? Have you taken the time to count them? Are you telling those who go behind you the meaning of the stones?

Prayer (from Joshua 4:24): Lord, by the power of Your Holy Spirit, help us to identify the stones that You have given to be a memorial, so that all the people of the earth might know that Your hand is powerful and they might always fear the Lord, their God. Amen.

Hoping for spring, for a world renewed
Looking for life on earth, hard and crude
Wanting promise to show itself true
Yearning to see in me more of You
Groaning relief from burdens of snow
Praying Your peace to once again know
Recalling grace to my knees I bow
Owning blessing beyond here and now
Accepting long winter's slow depart
Thanking eternal spring dwells in my heart

(Revelations 6 and 7)

Tribulation, death, famine, plague, a great earthquake. A blackened sun. Stars falling to the earth like figs falling from a tree on a windy day. The sky, rolled up like a scroll. Mountains and islands displaced.

Then, a call…to the rocks: "Fall on us and hide us from the face of him who sits on the throne and from the great wrath of the Lamb! For the great day of their wrath has come, and who can stand?" (Revelation 6:16b and 17).

A covering—a covering is needed for the shame, for the unworthiness. We know it. The One who sees us is coming. Who indeed can stand unashamed in the presence of this holy and just God? The one who can displace mountains and islands can certainly move the rocks that we might want to hide us in our darkness.

But wait, there *are* some standing. Many—too many to count. They are standing before the throne of God and the Lamb of God, His Son. They stand, and they are covered. They are covered, not by mountains and rocks, but by a robe made white by washing—not in bleach, but in blood. Ironic—stains removed by blood. The Lamb's blood—sacrificial blood—a sacrificial death, the price for life. Guilt, perfectly paid for. They have no shame, those who stand covered, just gratitude and praise; for they belong to the Lamb who has become their shepherd. More irony—the Lamb once sacrificed is now a shepherd, leading. This Shepherd-Lamb provides for all their needs. This

Shepherd-Lamb provides the robes to cover them. The angels sing, "In a loud voice they sang: Worthy is the Lamb, who was slain, to receive power and wealth and wisdom and strength and honor and glory and praise! Then I heard every creature in heaven and on earth and under the earth and on the sea, and all that is in them, singing: 'To him who sits on the throne and to the Lamb be praise and honor and glory and power for ever and ever!'" (Revelation 5:12–13).

Prayer: Lamb to Shepherd. Sacrifice to Savior. Provider of living water. Surely goodness and mercy has gone before us and follows us, and we will dwell in Your house forever. Thank You, Jesus, for all You are and all You have done, and thank You for my beautiful white robe!

The random melody of melancholy wind chimes
Join in chorus with
Colorful woodland birds gathering at the feeder,
Shattering the silence
On a cold winter day.
And a voice is heard
In the peaceful stillness.
The random thoughts of a drifting mind
Join in chorus with
An earnest prayer sent heavenward from a longing heart,
Shattering the silence
On a cold winter day.
And a voice is heard
In the peaceful stillness.

(Matthew 27:62–66; Matthew 28:1–5)

Jesus had died. His body was laid in a tomb. A rock was rolled in front of the entrance. It was finished. The darkness of His death—secured, contained, separated from mankind. But, of course, His death could not be separated from mankind. It was for mankind that He died. Some who accused Him of a life of deception sealed the tomb and stood guard, lest others take His body and claim He did what He said He would do: rise again. We know that those who accused Him of deception were the ones deceived, and when the earth quaked and the angel appeared, the deceived were presented with the truth, and they became as dead men.

That tomb that was sealed was not meant to stay sealed. Sometimes our hearts are like that tomb. We seal them up to protect our truth—our own perceptions. Our truth is deception if it is mis-aligned with God's truth. We try to protect our own truth against anyone who might try to expose it for what it is. We would like to keep Jesus dead in the tomb of our hearts. But Jesus is love, and Jesus is light; light always overcomes darkness. Jesus is truth, and truth can break the toughest seal. He is able to expose both the deceiver and the deceived. Are you willing to have the darkness and doom of impending death in your heart exposed to the one who can resurrect it to new life?

Do not be like those guards who were exposed to truth and exchanged it for a lie, rejecting it for a bribe and agreeing to become deceivers themselves. They sealed their own fate to darkness and death. Have you witnessed the resurrection of your Lord, the resurrection of your life? Have you seen the truth? Have you told the truth? If not, are you willing to?

Prayer: Lord, You have said You are the resurrection and the Life and that in believing in You, though we die, we will live. We pray that all who have witnessed the miracle of a broken seal have the courage to tell the truth about it.

(INSPIRED BY THE LIFE OF JACKIE DEKKER)

A voice of encouragement with echoes of love
A custom-made gift from God above
Ears ready to listen to whatever was shared
Never a doubt of how much she cared
Willing hands serving, with special touch
A gracious hostess that shared so much
Her laugh and smile, we still recall it so well
With every story she had to tell
All the cards that she sent, birthdays never to miss
Personal greetings, hugs, and a kiss
May all the love seeds that she worked so hard to sow
Bloom in our hearts, forever to grow

(JOHN 1:1; JOHN 12:49–50; ISAIAH 50:4; ISAIAH 55:10–13)

Winter may seem lifeless at times, but when we walk with God, there is always life. The life is in us, and it is in the seed that we sow. "In the beginning was the Word, and the Word was with God, and the Word was God" (John 1:1). This Word of God was spoken through the mouth of Jesus; this Word was Jesus. It is Jesus, and He is the word that sustains the weary. The Word, Jesus, was given to us, quickening us to life, to new life, to eternal life. The Word in us is being scattered around the world wherever God has placed us. God Himself, through the work of His Spirit, brings the seeds to life after using us as a means of dispersal. Like rain and snow from heaven fulfilling their purpose to water the earth and create new life, so it is with God's Word in us, which quenches our dry souls, giving us new life. In that life, we produce more seed as we share that Word, and God, in turn, quickens that seed to life. Just as plants disperse seeds in a variety of ways, so are we uniquely designed to be vehicles of dispersal throughout the world in our unique ways, in our unique setting, and in the time frame that He ordains. His Word of love in us changes the world, and His seed will not die.

Prayer: Help us to tend the soil of our hearts to the very end of our lives here on earth, Lord. Help us also to remove whatever is trying to choke out Your Word, Your life, in us—Your life spread through us. Give us an awareness of Your purpose wherever we are, whatever we are doing, regardless of our age, our gender, or our station in life. Help us live in the knowledge that we are who we are and that we are where we are so that we can bring the Word of life at this time, at this place, and to these people You have put in our life. May Your Word forever flourish, even as You have said in Luke 21:33: "Heaven and earth will pass away, but my words will never pass away." As You have said, so shall it be. Amen.

N*ow in Winter when this world's future looks bleak*
Your body and mind begin to grow weak
My love bridges hope from heaven to earth
For it's my sacrifice that proved your worth
When seasons have passed, and all things are made new
Still I'll forever dwell with you.

About the Author

JoAnn Dekker enjoys her walk with God in Indiana, where she is gratefully married to Jeff, her husband, friend, and encourager. Together, they live in thanks for their three daughters and son-in-laws, and their ten growing-up-unbelievably-fast grandchildren.

JoAnn works part time as a hospice nurse, trying to make the most of every opportunity to share the message of the love of Jesus—the One who "comforts us in all our troubles, so that we can comfort those in any trouble with the comfort we ourselves have received" (2 Corinthians 1:4).